Teaching English Grammar in Asian Contexts

This book guides teachers, teacher educators and pre-service student teachers on using grammar as a pedagogical tool for meaning making, linking grammar as a meaning-making resource to literacy development. When grammar is meaningfully linked to literacy skills such as reading and writing, there is contextualised teaching of grammar.

The authors thoroughly explore key concepts in grammar, including grammar as structure and grammar as choice. They illuminate these concepts by analysing a range of authentic texts from Asian contexts, showing how specific grammar features are purposefully used to convey meaning. Examples and illustrations of teaching ideas and materials focusing on contextualised teaching of grammar, including lesson plans, activity outlines, worksheets and teaching strategies, are contributed by current teacher practitioners who have tried out these ideas in their language classes. These teacher practitioners also share their reflections on how these ideas have worked in their classes.

As a result, this book is an indispensable resource for teachers, teacher educators, pre-service teachers of English as both a first language and a second or foreign language, as well as anyone who is interested in harnessing the power of grammar to enhance English language teaching and literacy development.

Dr Christine Anita Xavier is a teacher educator and researcher in the English Language and Literature department at the National Institute of Education, Nanyang Technological University, Singapore. She teaches courses on grammar and linguistics within the pre-service, higher degree and in-service programmes. Her research focuses on the intersections between theory and practice in the areas of pedagogical grammar and English language variation and use.

Dr Alexius Chia is a teacher educator and researcher in the English Language and Literature department at the National Institute of Education, Nanyang Technological University, Singapore. He teaches courses on language teaching methods, including teaching grammar, to pre-service and leadership programmes. Before he joined NIE, he was a Head of Department/English Language and Literature at two local Singapore schools. His research focuses on curriculum implementation, multiliteracies, multimodality and teacher professional learning.

Teaching English Grammar in Asian Contexts
Making Meaning with Grammar

Christine Anita Xavier and Alexius Chia

LONDON AND NEW YORK

Designed cover image: @Getty Image

First published 2025
by Routledge
4 Park Square, Milton Park, Abingdon, Oxon OX14 4RN

and by Routledge
605 Third Avenue, New York, NY 10158

Routledge is an imprint of the Taylor & Francis Group, an informa business

© 2025 Christine Anita Xavier and Alexius Chia

The right of Christine Anita Xavier and Alexius Chia to be identified as authors of this work has been asserted in accordance with sections 77 and 78 of the Copyright, Designs and Patents Act 1988.

All rights reserved. No part of this book may be reprinted or reproduced or utilised in any form or by any electronic, mechanical, or other means, now known or hereafter invented, including photocopying and recording, or in any information storage or retrieval system, without permission in writing from the publishers.

Trademark notice: Product or corporate names may be trademarks or registered trademarks, and are used only for identification and explanation without intent to infringe.

British Library Cataloguing-in-Publication Data
A catalogue record for this book is available from the British Library

ISBN: 978-1-032-18734-1 (hbk)
ISBN: 978-1-032-18732-7 (pbk)
ISBN: 978-1-003-25596-3 (ebk)

DOI: 10.4324/9781003255963

Typeset in Galliard
by Apex CoVantage, LLC

To our families – your unwavering support, patience and encouragement made this journey possible. We could not have completed this book without your love and understanding. Thank you for believing in us and for always being our greatest champions.

Contents

List of Figures   *viii*
Acknowledgements   *ix*

1 Introduction   1

2 Words and Word Classes   9

3 Nouns and Noun Phrases   34

4 Verbs and Verb Phrases   51

5 Clauses and Sentences   84

6 Grammatical Functions   100

7 Cohesion and Coherence   121

8 Conclusion   149

Index   *158*

Figures

2.1 Categories of nouns — 10
3.1 Structure of a noun phrase — 46
7.1 Anaphoric and cataphoric references in *A True Good Thai* — 143
8.1 The role and place of grammar in teaching and learning — 150

Acknowledgements

The case studies shared in the book are a result of a study funded by Singapore's Ministry of Education (MOE) under the Education Research Funding Programme (PG 07/22 CAX) and administered by the National Institute of Education (NIE), Nanyang Technological University, Singapore. Any opinions, findings, and conclusions or recommendations expressed in this material are those of the authors and do not necessarily reflect the views of the Singapore MOE and NIE. This research has received clearance from the NTU-Institutional Review Board [IRB-2021-544]. We also acknowledge the work that our Research Assistant, Theresa Belmonte, has put in to assist us with the transcription and coding of the data.

We would like to extend our heartfelt gratitude to our amazing teacher-collaborators who bravely embarked on this incredible journey of discovery with us. Alvin, HingMH, Gajen, Felice, TAnne, Tasha, Norton, Masyita, Nathan, and Said – your boundless enthusiasm and tireless dedication have truly inspired us. We are deeply thankful for all the hard work you have poured into this project.

Special thanks to the wonderful writers of the Asian texts we featured in our book – Edmund Lim and Sunisa Manning (published by Epigram Books), Carmelita C. Ballesteros, David T.K. Wong, Lee Su Kim, Chia Ah Hang, Fitri Kurniawan and Dennis Yeo. We are profoundly grateful for your incredible generosity in granting permission to use your works in the teachers' resource materials and in this book. Your support has been invaluable, and we are honoured to have your contributions enriching this journey.

1 Introduction

About this Book

This book sets out to make explicit how grammar could be used as a pedagogical tool for making meaning, linking grammar as a meaning-making resource to literacy development. When grammar is meaningfully linked to literacy skills like reading and writing development, there is contextualised teaching of grammar. Such an integrated approach to teaching language adopts a descriptive view of grammar, where relations between grammatical choices and the meanings they construct are surfaced. This view sees grammar as choice, as a meaning-making resource. This contrasts with the prescriptive view of grammar, where accuracy of grammatical structures is the emphasis. The prescriptive view of grammar is usually adopted when grammar teaching is done in isolation. So, while the descriptive view of grammar emphasises grammar as choice, the prescriptive view of grammar emphasises grammar as structure. Carter and McCarthy, however, stress that 'the grammar of choice is as important as the grammar of structure' (2006, p. 7).

It is indeed true that both the grammar of structure and the grammar of choice are important. To be able to talk about grammar as choice, as a meaning-making resource, we need to have an adequate knowledge of grammar as structure. As such, this book aims to be a bridge between grammar of structure and grammar of choice. It covers essential grammar content knowledge (grammar as structure) and illustrates how grammatical choices are made within grammatical structures in authentic texts. Additionally, this book shares teaching ideas and materials from practising English language teachers situated in the Asian context, particularly, Singapore, who explored contextualised teaching of grammar in their primary and secondary English language classrooms with the aim of developing their students' literacy skills.

Expanding on the structure of the book, it covers grammar content at the word, phrase, clause, sentence and text levels. Each area of grammar emphasises both grammar as structure and grammar as choice. To illustrate how grammar as structure can be used as grammar as choice in reading and writing, authentic texts are analysed in terms of the purposeful use of specific grammar features to express meaning in these texts. These authentic texts, primarily excerpts

DOI: 10.4324/9781003255963-1

from various sources set in Asian contexts, are chosen as relevant and appealing to the target audience. Examples and illustrations of teaching ideas and materials – including lesson plans, activity outlines, worksheets and teaching strategies – contributed by English language teachers who explored integrating grammar as a meaning-making resource in their classes are also included. Additionally, reflections by these teachers on the effectiveness of this approach to grammar teaching in their classes are also shared. This book is thus useful to teacher educators, teachers, pre-service teachers and anyone who is interested in the place of grammar in English language teaching and in literacy development.

Views of Grammar Adopted in this Book

There are generally two views of grammar: the prescriptive and the descriptive. The particular view of grammar adopted has implications for how grammar is taught and learnt in the English language classroom, and consequently on literacy development. The **prescriptive view of grammar** centres on grammar rules, with a preoccupation with how language *should* be used. Such a view of grammar prioritises accuracy of grammar use and so is error-focused – focusing on either the avoidance of errors or the remediation of errors. When such a view of grammar is adopted in the classroom, grammar teaching focuses on grammar rules, errors, and grammar drills, disconnected from meaningful contextual application. Grammatical structures are taught in isolation, emphasising grammar for its own sake. This prescriptive view of grammar primarily confines the role of grammar to the correct use of grammatical structures. Consequently, in classrooms where this view of grammar is embraced, grammar and literacy skills like reading and writing are typically taught as separate entities.

On the contrary, the **descriptive view of grammar** focuses on the usage of language across diverse contexts. While the prescriptive view highlights the importance of adhering to grammatical rules, the descriptive approach underscores grammatical choices, exploring linguistic possibilities within language. This perspective places importance on how grammatical choices construct various meanings within text. Consequently, grammar is perceived as a resource for meaning creation within textual contexts. When implementing the descriptive view of grammar in the classroom, grammar teaching is contextualised within literacy skills. This integrated approach ensures that grammar and literacy skills are taught in tandem, emphasising their interconnectedness and purposeful application in literacy development.

Research on grammar teaching underscores longstanding debates regarding the role of grammar in literacy development. Within the realm of writing development, one key argument revolves around whether grammar teaching significantly impacts writing skills. Jones et al. (2012) assert that studies and reviews suggesting minimal benefits from grammar teaching (for example, Andrews et al., 2004, 2006; Bateman & Zidonis, 1966; Elley et al.,

1976; Hinkel, 2008) often examine grammar and writing as separate entities, attempting to establish connections between them afterward. They note that in such studies, 'isolated grammar lessons are taught as part of a curriculum programme in grammar, and the writing measures used to draw empirical conclusions are produced in a different teaching context' (p. 1242). These grammar lessons usually adopt a prescriptive approach, focusing on grammatical structures such as parsing of sentences.

Myhill et al. (2012b) argue that such disjointed approaches fail to positively impact writing development due to a lack of integration between grammar and writing. They advocate for a contextualised teaching approach that embraces a descriptive view of grammar, emphasising grammar as choice. This perspective aligns with previous studies (for example, Calkins, 1980; DiStefano & Killion, 1984; Kolln, 1981; Weaver, 1996) which highlight the importance of establishing connections between linguistic choices and the meanings they convey.

The notion of contextualised grammar teaching finds support in a large-scale study led by Debra Myhill and her team as reported in Myhill et al. (2012a) and Jones et al. (2012). This study explored the impact of explicit, contextualised grammar teaching on students' writing performance. The findings indicate that when grammar is taught within the context of writing lessons, it positively influences students' writing development, as grammar is meaningfully linked to writing demands. Grammar is thus perceived as a resource for creating meaning and 'an enabling element in writing development' (Myhill et al., 2012a, p. 162). This approach empowers learners to recognise the dynamic force of grammar, enabling them to make informed grammatical choices within diverse textual contexts.

Contextualising this Book

Language teaching in many Asian contexts often adheres to a predominantly static, prescriptive approach to grammar instruction. Consequently, there is a strong focus on teaching grammar as a separate entity, focusing primarily on its structure (form). This traditional approach manifests in teaching methods such as drill and practice, fill-in-the-blank exercises and multiple-choice questions, devoid of real-world contexts. Despite research indicating the effectiveness of a more contextualised approach to the teaching of grammar, many Asian classrooms have yet to adopt this practice. Transitioning from a static to a dynamic approach to grammar teaching, where learners are made aware of purposeful choices in terms of grammatical usage, can lead to more effective and meaningful learning outcomes.

However, the available books and resources which examine language functionally, particularly in terms of grammar, predominantly stem from the Australian contexts that embrace Systemic Functional Linguistics (SFL) (for example, Halliday and Matthiessen, 2004). SFL may not be widely familiar to many teachers in Asia, where grammar instruction tends to be more form-focused, emphasising a structural approach. In addition, adopting SFL would necessitate a significant overhaul of the entire English Language curriculum, particularly in countries like Singapore, where a new set of metalanguage would need to be adopted.

Therefore, there is a pressing need for a resource that explicitly connects grammar as structure (form) and grammar as choice (function) through content, analysis of texts, and teaching ideas. This book endeavours to bridge the gap between form and function by using the metalanguage of form-focused grammar as a tool for meaning making across a variety of authentic contexts.

This book stands apart from other functional grammar resources in its unique focus on authentic texts derived from Asian contexts. Unlike many functional grammar books that primarily analyse excerpts from Western cultural contexts such as Australia, the United Kingdom or the United States, our book ensures relevance and familiarity to teacher practitioners and students in Asia. As one of our Singapore teacher-collaborators shared, 'I was very interested in your book idea when you said you wanted to localise material . . . We currently use a lot of stuff adapted from the UK curriculum . . . but I believe in authentic texts and fresh examples so that students see the relevance to their daily lives!' Incorporating culturally relevant texts that resonate with learners' personal experiences and cultural heritage enhances contextualised learning, thus facilitating the exploration of grammar as a tool for meaning making within these texts.

Drawing from Ladson-Billings (1992), culturally relevant teaching is the kind of teaching that uses 'student culture as the basis for helping students understand themselves and others, structure social interactions, and conceptualise knowledge' (p. 314). We express our heartfelt gratitude to our esteemed authors, whose contributions from diverse Asian contexts have enriched the content of this book. Their generosity in allowing us to feature their work is deeply appreciated.

Another distinctive feature of this book is its use of a teacher's voice to convey grammar knowledge in simple and relatable ways, catering to educators who may lack linguistic expertise. Additionally, the inclusion of case studies from current teacher practitioners strengthens the book by illustrating the practical application of grammar concepts in the development of literacy skills. These case studies, arising from a theory-practice partnership between the authors – both teacher educators and researchers – and 10 teacher-collaborators from primary and secondary schools in Singapore, provide valuable insights into effective teaching strategies. At this juncture, we would like to extend our sincere thanks to these 10 wonderful teacher-collaborators, all accomplished practitioners (who, for ethical reasons, must remain unnamed and so, are referred to in the book by pseudonyms). They wholeheartedly embraced this endeavour. Their willingness to share their time, resources and insights has been invaluable. We are immensely grateful for their contributions, which have greatly enhanced the richness and practicality of this book.

This collaborative effort resulted in an innovative, contextually relevant approach to grammar teaching for literacy development in Singapore English language classrooms. Initiated as an intervention action research project, the endeavour emerged from a recognition of learner needs. The teachers observed that while their students seemed to do well in isolated grammar tasks like drills and worksheets, they struggled to apply grammar effectively in literacy tasks, such as writing. This realisation prompted a departure from traditional practices, shifting towards a more integrated approach that emphasises the role of grammar as a meaning-making resource within literacy contexts.

The action research project comprised several key steps:

(i) **Teachers identifying their learners' needs**. Prompted to reflect on their learners' literacy requirements, teachers pinpointed specific areas requiring additional support, such as reading or writing improvement, enabling targeted interventions.

(ii) **Teachers identifying their own professional needs**. Teachers evaluated their own learning needs, identifying gaps in grammar content knowledge and pedagogical content knowledge essential for engaging in their classroom interventions effectively.

(iii) **Teacher educators conducting targeted professional development sessions**. Tailored professional development sessions covering pertinent grammar and pedagogical content knowledge were provided to support the teachers in their understanding of contextualised grammar teaching. These equipped them with the necessary grammar content knowledge and pedagogical strategies to integrate grammar instruction into their literacy lessons.

(iv) **Teachers revising a unit of work or lesson which they had identified**. Collaborating with the teacher educators, teachers redesigned these units or lesson/s focusing on literacy development, incorporating lesson plans, teaching materials and pedagogical approaches. The aim was to integrate the teaching of grammar as a meaning-making resource within a contextualised learning framework, including the deliberate inclusion of authentic Asian texts as model or rich texts.

(v) **Teachers teaching the revised units or lessons**. The teachers proceeded to teach the revised units and lessons, putting into practice the integrated approach to grammar instruction.

(vi) **Teacher educators conducting post-lesson interviews**. Following lesson enactment, the teacher educators interviewed teachers to gather insights into the modified teaching and learning processes and their impact on enhancing students' literacy skills development.

(vii) **Teachers reflecting on the impact of the process**. The teachers engaged in reflection, evaluating their own professional growth and the learning outcomes achieved by their students as a result of the interventions.

The interviews and reflections underscore the efficacy of this innovative approach to contextualised grammar teaching for literacy development, yielding benefits for both the teachers in terms of teacher professional growth and their learners in terms of learner literacy enhancement. However, this new approach also presented challenges to both teachers and learners. A more comprehensive discussion of these benefits and challenges will be provided in the concluding chapter of this book.

Structure of this Book

The structure of this book is consistent across all chapters, apart from the introductory and concluding chapters. It begins by presenting the grammar content knowledge of the respective grammar feature(s) (grammar as structure). This is followed by analyses illustrating the purposeful use of the respective grammar feature(s) in authentic texts to convey meaning (grammar as choice). Subsequently, the chapter provides examples and illustrations from teacher practitioners who have implemented teaching strategies integrating the respective grammar feature(s) as a tool for meaning making in their English language classrooms. These lessons used authentic Asian texts as model texts, with a specific focus on supporting students' literacy development. Additionally, the teachers share reflections on the effectiveness of these strategies in their classes. The concluding chapter wraps up the book by proposing a model of English language teaching and learning that includes grammar integration. It also shares some benefits and challenges of adopting a contextualised approach to the teaching of grammar for literacy development for both teachers and students.

To demonstrate the intentional application of specific grammar features in authentic texts to convey meaning throughout Chapters 2–6, excerpts from the introductory chapter, 'The Fall', from *Where's Grandma* by Edmund Lim, are used. This book, set in Singapore, narrates the story about a boy, Luke, grappling with his grandmother's battle with Alzheimer's disease. Additionally, the book's concluding chapter, 'Not Goodbye' will serve as the focal point for analysis and discussion in Chapter 7 on Cohesion and Coherence. The complete introductory chapter, 'The Fall', is provided below for reference.

'The Fall' from *Where's Grandma?* (by Edmund Lim)

'Grandma, where are the keys?' I asked.

'They're in the second drawer of the cabinet,' she replied, smiling.

I knew I could count on Grandma's help. I went to the cabinet, pulled open the drawer and rummaged through the contents.

'I found them! Let's go to the park now.'

'Alright, give me a minute,' she said as she shifted to get her walking stick.

Thin and tall, Grandma walked slowly but steadily to the door. I held her arm as we walked towards the lift and kept the door open as Grandma tottered inside.

For the past month, we had not been to the playground. Instead, we went to the neighbourhood park. For fifteen minutes every day, we would stroll together so that Grandma could get some fresh air and light exercise.

Grandma has always stayed with us. She lives with Dad, Mum and me in our four-room apartment in Toa Payoh. Grandma passed away when I was a baby. In the day, Grandma used to take care of me because Dad and Mum had to work.

Grandma was a wonderful cook. She made lunch for both of us. I could eat two bowls of Grandma's delicious potato curry. I will never forget the smell of the curry and her tasty, chewy home-made ang ku kueh – absolutely mouth-watering.

When I was little, Grandma took me to the nearby playground every evening. She would hold my hand as we walked through the void decks and car parks. When we approached the playground, I would dash to the swings and then feel Grandma's warm palms pushing my back as I soared into the sky.

Grandma would then sit on the bench and keep an eye on me. Sometimes, when I did not have a friend to play with, she would sit on the other end of the see-saw, her wrinkled, dry feet bracing herself as we bounced up and down.

Grandma would also be around to help when I fell ill. She would check if I was alright and encourage me to get up on my feet. If there was a wound, she would quickly take out her handkerchief to wipe away the blood.

Grandma did only take me to the playground. When I entered Primary ne, she took me to school too. Hand in hand, we would walk to school which was on the far side of the housing estate. While we walked, we would talk about the things we planned to do that day. I liked it best when she took out her special album of black and white photos and told me stories about her childhood in a small kampong in Penang.

Every morning at the school gate, Grandma would give me a big warm hug and say, 'Study hard, Luke. See you later.' At the end of the school day, she would be at the gate waiting for me. That was my dear Grandma.

Things changed after the fall. It was Grandma who fell. While coming out of the toilet, Grandma slipped and crashed onto the floor. Kaboonk!

I dashed into the toilet. Grandma was groaning softly. Blood oozed from a deep gash on her forehead. She had also sprained her left ankle. That happened almost two months ago. Although Grandma recovered, she walks with a slight limp and a walking stick.

Grandma's fall was just the beginning.

References

Andrews, R., Torgerson, C., Beverton, S., Locke, T., Low, G., Robinson, A., & Zhu, D. (2004). *The Effect of Grammar Teaching (Syntax) in English on 5 to 16 Year Olds' Accuracy and Quality in Written Composition.* EPPI-Centre, Social Science Research Unit, Institute of Education.

Andrews, R., Torgerson, C., Beverton, S., Freeman, A., Locke, T., Low, G., Robinson, A., & Zhu, D. (2006). The effect of grammar teaching on writing development. *British Educational Research Journal, 32*(1) 39–55.

Bateman, D.R., & Zidonis, F.J. (1966). *The Effect of a Study of Transformational Grammar on the Writing of Ninth and Tenth Graders*. National Council of Teachers of English.

Carter, R., & McCarthy, M. (2006). *Cambridge Grammar of English*. Cambridge University Press.

Calkins, L. M. (1980). When children want to punctuate: Basic skills belong in context. *Language Arts, 57*, 567–573.

DiStefano, P., & Killion, J. (1984). Assessing writing skills through a process approach. *English Education, 11*, 98–101.

Elley, W.B., Barham, I.H., Lamb, H., & Wylie, M. (1976). The role of grammar in a secondary school curriculum. *Research in the Teaching of English, 10*(1), 5–21.

Halliday, M.A.K. & Matthiessen, C.M.I.M. (2004). *An Introduction to Functional Grammar* (3rd ed.). Routledge. https://doi.org/10.4324/9780203783771.

Hinkel, E. (2008) Teaching grammar in writing classes: Tenses and cohesion. In E. Hinkel & S. Fotos (eds), *New Perspectives in Grammar Teaching in Second Language Classrooms*. Routledge.

Jones, S., Myhill, D.A. & Bailey, T. (2012). Grammar for writing? An investigation of the effects of contextualized grammar teaching on students' writing. *Reading and Writing, 26*, 1241–1263.

Kolln, M. (1981). Closing the books on alchemy. *College Composition and Communication, 31*, 139–151.

Ladson-Billings, G. (1992). Reading between the lines and beyond the pages: A culturally relevant approach to literacy teaching. *Theory Into Practice, 31*(4), 312–320.

Lim, E. (2012). *Where's Grandma?* Epigram Books.

Myhill, D.A., Jones, S.M., Lines, H., & Watson, A. (2012a). Re-thinking grammar: The impact of embedded grammar teaching on students' writing and students' metalinguistic understanding. *Research Papers in Education, 27*(2), 139–166.

Myhill, D.A., Lines, H., & Watson, A. (2012b). Making meaning with grammar: A repertoire of possibilities. *English in Australia, 47*(3), 29–38.

Weaver, C. (1996). Teaching grammar in the context of writing. *The English Journal, 85*(7), 15–24.

2   Words and Word Classes

What are Word Classes?

Let's begin at the word level, by looking at word classes. What are word classes? Word classes, also known as parts of speech, are categories of words which have similar properties in terms of meaning, form and function. There are eight (or more, depending on different grammatical systems) word classes and these are nouns, verbs, adjectives, adverbs, pronouns, determiners, prepositions and conjunctions.

Why study word classes? Word classes are important because the English language is strict about the order of words in a phrase, clause or sentence to express intended meaning. The order of words as building blocks in a phrase, clause or sentence is dependent on the word classes of these words. For example, in a noun phrase, the determiner comes before the adjective, and the adjective comes before the head noun (det<adjective<head noun), as in the noun phrase *the sly fox* where *the* is the determiner, *sly* is the adjective and *fox* is the head noun. One is not able to order these words differently to create a meaningful noun phrase, for example, **sly the fox* (note: * is used in the book to mark ungrammatical structures), which does not make sense. As such, knowing the word class of a word helps us to form accurate, meaningful phrases, clauses and sentences.

Words may be categorised into different word classes based on meaning, form and function. Traditionally, words were grouped into these word classes based purely on their meaning. However, this manner of categorisation is not very helpful as the core meaning of words may be the same, like for example, *happy* and *happiness* which are both positive feelings, but these words have different forms and functions. Merely knowing the meaning of words will not help us decide how we should shape the word (form) or where we should place the word within a phrase, clause or sentence to fulfil a particular role (function). As such, we can only use words meaningfully in context if we understand the properties of words in terms of meaning, form and function.

DOI: 10.4324/9781003255963-2

The *meaning* of a word provides you with a sense of the word. The *form* of a word is about how the word looks like – the presence of prefixes (word beginnings) or suffixes (word endings), or the prefixes or suffixes that the word can take. The *function* of the word can be considered from two perspectives– one, where the word occurs in a phrase, clause or sentence in relation to its neighbouring words and two, what role it plays in the context of the phrase, clause or sentence.

So, to decide which word class a word belongs to, we can ask the following questions in relation to the various word classes:

1. Does this word have similar meanings to words in a particular word class?
2. Does this word have similar word forms to words in a particular word class?
3. Does this word occur in a similar place within a phrase, clause or sentence as words in a particular word class?
4. Does this word play a similar role within the context of a phrase, clause or sentence as words in a particular word class?

Before illustrating how we can determine the word class of a word, let's familiarise ourselves with the distinctive properties of the various word classes.

Nouns (N)

Meaning

Words that are nouns label objects, people, places, concepts and activities, like *toy, John, playground, kindness* and *picnic*. As you can gather from the examples, there are different types of nouns. We can categorise nouns as illustrated in Figure 2.1.

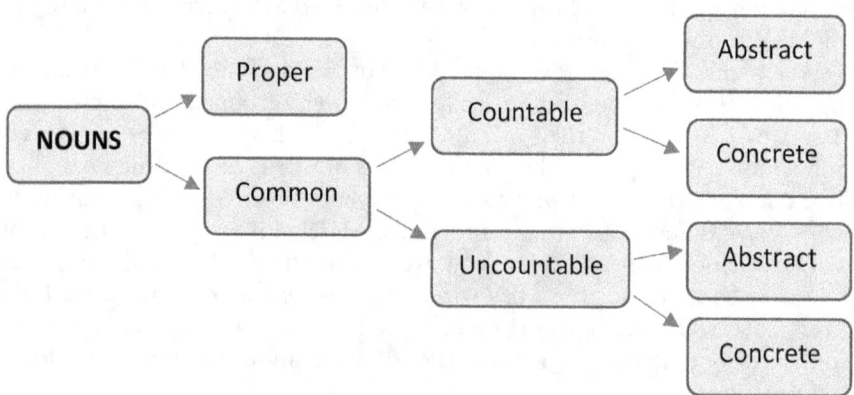

Figure 2.1 Categories of nouns.

- Proper nouns – These are names of particular people or groups (like *Min*, *Mary Anne*, *Mr. Syed*, and *One Direction*), places (like *Singapore*, *Borobudur*, *Mount Kinabalu*, and *The Forbidden City*), times (like *Thursday* and *January*) and occasions/events/festivals (like *Chinese New Year*, *Deepavali*, *Songkran* and *Lantern Festival*). The following are some points to take note about proper nouns:
  - Proper nouns start with a capital letter.
  - Proper nouns typically do not take plural forms. However, there are exceptions – for example, when referring to a number of persons with the same name, as in *All the <u>Alans</u> I know are talented*.
  - Proper nouns typically do not take determiners. However, there are exceptions – for example, when the determiner is part of the name of the place, as in *<u>The</u> Forbidden City* or when the proper noun is not used to refer to a specific person but a representation of this person, as in, *I saw <u>a</u> Van Gogh at the exhibition*. Here, the reference is to a Van Gogh painting and not to Van Gogh, the painter.
- Common nouns – These are names for general (and not specific) things, ideas, people, places and times. The following are some points to take note about common nouns:
  - Common nouns do not start with a capital letter.
  - Common nouns typically take determiners (for example, *<u>an</u> eraser*, *<u>the</u> pencils* and *<u>those</u> rulers*).
  - Common nouns can be countable or uncountable (elaborated on below).
  - Common nouns can be concrete or abstract (elaborated on below).
- Countable and uncountable nouns – Common nouns can be countable or uncountable.
  - Countable nouns can be distinguished and counted (for example, *one spoon* vs *five spoons*). There are some points to take note about countable nouns:
    - Countable nouns may take both singular and plural forms (for example, *one pen* vs *ten pens*).
    - Countable nouns may agree with both singular and plural verbs, depending on whether the nouns are singular or plural (for example, *<u>One student is</u> absent today* vs *<u>Three students are</u> absent today*).
    - Singular countable nouns cannot stand alone without a determiner. For example, it is ungrammatical to say **I bought shirt*. We will need to add a determiner before the singular noun shirt, to say, for example, *I bought a shirt* or *I bought that shirt*.
    - Plural countable nouns occur with specific quantifiers like *a few*, *several* and *many* that help to distinguish these countable nouns (for example, *a few cars, many books*)

- Uncountable nouns (otherwise known as non-count or mass nouns) cannot be distinguished and counted. For example, the uncountable nouns *water* and *furniture* cannot be counted – it is ungrammatical to say *two waters or *two furnitures. The following are some points to take note about uncountable nouns:
  - Uncountable nouns take only the singular form. For example, it is ungrammatical to say *equipments or *informations. To quantify uncountable nouns, partitive nouns are used. An example of a partitive noun is *piece*. As such, it would be grammatical to say *The three <u>pieces</u> of information were provided*. Other examples of partitive nouns are *tablespoon* (for example, *three <u>tablespoons</u> of sugar*), *cup* (for example, *two <u>cups</u> of rice*) and *slice* for example, *five <u>slices</u> of bread*).
  - Uncountable nouns only agree with the singular verb. For example, even when referring to more than one piece of furniture, it is only grammatical to say *The furniture is old* and not **The furnitures are old*. Here, it would be possible to use a partitive noun and say *The two <u>pieces</u> of furniture are old*.
  - Uncountable nouns may take a determiner or not. For example, it is grammatical to say either *She spilled <u>water</u> on the floor* or *She spilled <u>some water</u> on the floor*.
  - Uncountable nouns occur with specific quantifiers like *some*, *little* and *much* (for example, *little oil, some sugar*)

Form

Nouns typically take specific suffixes like the plural *-s* suffix in *toys* to signal the plural and the possessive *-'s* suffix in *John's* to create possessive forms. It is important to note that the spelling of plural nouns and possessive nouns can differ depending on various factors like the word endings of these nouns, and whether these nouns are regular or irregular nouns. Other typical suffixes attached to words that are nouns include *-ment*, *-hood*, *-ation/-tion*, *-ness*, *-an* and *-ism*.

Function

Nouns usually join determiners and adjectives (and possibly other nouns) in a particular word order to construct noun phrases. The noun will be the head of the noun phrase, and determiners and adjectives may come before the head noun (det>adj>head noun) to modify the head noun as premodifiers to the head noun. For example, *the fast car* is a noun phrase with *car* as the head noun and *the* as the determiner and *fast* as the adjective. Do note that there may also be postmodifiers, like preposition phrases, which come immediately after the head noun in a noun phrase to modify the head noun. For example, *the fast car in the right lane,* is a noun phrase with the preposition phrase *in the right lane* postmodifying the head noun *car*. These noun phrases (sometimes just comprising the head noun, as the premodifiers and the postmodifiers may be optional) can play a variety of roles in sentences. They may be subjects, objects, complements or adverbials in a sentence depending on the context.

Verbs (V)

Meaning

Words that are verbs express actions or states of being. Verbs may be broadly categorised according to their meaning – action verbs, linking verbs, saying verbs, sensing verbs and mental verbs (see Alsagoff, 2023), and examples are *walk, am, shout, hear* and *think* respectively. These five categories will be elaborated on in Chapter 4. Please do note here that this is only one way of categorising verbs according to their meaning. For example, Michael Halliday, a well-known systemic functional grammarian, proposes six categories of verbs (material, mental, relational, verbal, existential and behavioural) according to their meaning (Halliday & Matthiessen, 2004).

Form

Verbs usually take on six forms: the base (for example, *walk, write*), the third person singular present tense usually marked by the suffix -*s* (for example, *walks, writes*), the past tense usually marked by the suffix -*ed* (for example, *walked, wrote*), the progressive or the continuous -*ing* participle (for example, *walking, writing*), the perfect -*ed/en* participle (for example, *walked, written*) and the passive -*ed/-en* participle (for example, *walked, written*). The verb forms may vary depending on whether these words are regular or irregular verbs. In the examples given, the verb *walk* is a regular verb and the verb *write* is an irregular verb. Please do note, however, that the copula verb *be* in English has eight different forms and these are *be, am, is, are, was, were, been* and *being*.

Function

Verbs may be main (lexical) or auxiliary (helping) verbs. Main verbs may have primary (for example, *be* and *have*) or modal (for example, *will, can* and *may*) auxiliaries precede them, forming a verb phrase. For example, *will be walking* is a verb phrase comprising the modal auxiliary *will*, the primary auxiliary *be* and the main verb *walking*. In a verb phrase, the main verb is obligatory to express an action or a state of being and the auxiliaries which provide additional grammatical information like modality and aspect are optional. It is important to note that other grammars may define the verb phrase as the main verb together with the auxiliaries, plus whatever else comes after the verb(s) in a clause but in this book, the verb phrase only consists of verbs. A verb phrase plays a central and necessary role in a clause to express an action or state of being. The verb phrase typically comes after the subject of a clause and it may be modified by adverbials (that may take the form of adverbs, preposition phrases, clauses and others).

Adjectives (Adj)

Meaning

Words that are adjectives describe the appearance or the quality of nouns and pronouns (see more on nouns above and more on pronouns below) like *rich*, *high*, *clever* and *little*.

Form

Adjectives can have specific suffixes like *-ful*, *-able*, *-al* and *-ious*. The use of a number of these suffixes converts nouns and verbs into adjectives. For example, the noun *hope* becomes the adjective *hopeful* with the addition of the suffix *-ful*, and the verb *teach* becomes the adjective *teachable* with the addition of the suffix *-able*. There is also a group of adjectives known as participial adjectives which are formed by the addition of the *-ing* progressive/continuous participle suffix and the *-ed/en* perfect participle suffix (for example, the adjectives *interesting* and *broken* in *the interesting book* and *the broken vase*). Another point to note on the form of adjectives is that gradable adjectives take on the comparative and superlative forms (please note that not all adjectives are gradable, as some adjectives are non-gradable). One- or two-syllable words that are regular, gradable adjectives take the suffixes *-er* and *-est* to form the comparative and superlative forms respectively. For example, the regular one-syllable adjective *sweet* has the comparative form *sweeter* with the *-er*, and the superlative form *sweetest* with the *-est*. If these regular, gradable adjectives are words of three or more syllables, the adverb *more* is used to form the comparative and the adverb *most* is used to form the superlative. For example, comparative and superlative forms of the regular, three-syllable adjective *beautiful* are formed with the use of the adverbs *more* and *most* respectively – *more beautiful* and *most beautiful*. If the gradable adjectives are irregular adjectives, then these have irregular comparative and superlative forms. For example, the irregular adjective *good* has the irregular comparative *better* and the superlative *best*.

Function

Adjectives may appear within a noun phrase (either before or after the head noun), or outside the noun phrase, following a linking verb. These words are labelled according to where they appear within a noun phrase or a clause. Adjectives that appear before the head noun in a noun phrase are called attributive adjectives. For example, in the noun phrase *the big book*, the attributive adjective *big* modifies the head noun *book*. The adjectives that appear after the head noun in a noun phrase are called postpositive adjectives. For example, in the noun phrase *the president elect*, the postpositive adjective *elect* modifies the head noun *president*. Those adjectives that appear outside a noun phrase, after a linking verb (for example, the verb *be*) are called predicative adjectives. For example, in the sentence *The girl is helpful*, the predicative adjective *helpful* comes after the linking verb *is* to modify the noun phrase *the girl*. So, words that are adjectives describe or modify nouns and pronouns. These adjectives, in turn, can be premodified by adverbs, to form adjective phrases (for example, *extremely glad*, where *extremely* is the adverb and *glad* is the adjective). An adjective can also be postmodified by a preposition phrase that acts as a complement to complete the meaning of the adjective (for example, <u>*Tom is happy with the gift*</u> where the preposition phrase *with the gift* modifies the adjective *happy* here). Adjectives or adjective phrases may be complements or adverbials in a sentence depending on the context.

Adverbs (Adv)

Meaning

Words that are adverbs most frequently answer the questions of 'when', 'where' and 'how' of an action or state. In other words, adverbs typically add information of time, place and manner to the verb or verb phrase. Examples of these adverbs are as follows:

- adverbs of time – These convey when, how long or how often an action or state happened. For example, the adverb *tomorrow* in *Mr Said will teach us tomorrow* adds information of when to the action or verb phrase *will teach*. Other examples of these adverbs are *just, eventually, soon, usually* and *daily*.
- adverbs of place – These convey where an action or state happened. For example, the adverb *there* in *We found the scrawny kitten there* adds information of place to the action or verb phrase *found*. Other examples of adverbs of place are *here, nearby, downstairs* and *outside*.
- adverbs of manner – These convey how or the way an action or state happened. For example, the adverb *strongly* in *Ram strongly believes in the importance of recycling* adds information of how to the state or verb phrase *believes*. Other examples of adverbs of manner are *greedily, well, happily, fast* and *carefully*.

Form

Adverbs typically take on the *-ly* suffix, and are usually referred to as *–ly* words. Do bear in mind, though, that there are several adjectives which also end with the *–ly* suffix and examples of these include *friendly, miserly, manly* and *elderly*. There are also numerous adverbs which do not take on the *-ly* suffix and these include adverbs like *well, fast* and *tomorrow* as mentioned above.

Function

Besides modifying verbs, adverbs perform several other functions like the following:

- Adverbs may modify other adverbs to form adverb phrases. An example of such an adverb phrase is *very quickly* in *Mazlan walked <u>very quickly</u>* where the adverb *very* premodifies the head adverb *quickly* to intensify this head

adverb. The adverb phrase then ultimately modifies the verb *walked* to convey the intensity or degree (how) at which this action took place.
- Adverbs may modify adjectives in an adjective phrase. Examples of such adjective phrases are <u>*usually noisy*</u> and <u>*strangely silent*</u> in *The <u>usually noisy</u> class was <u>strangely quiet</u> that day.* The adverb *usually* premodifies the adjective *noisy* to convey the frequency (when) at which the class is noisy and the adverb *strangely* premodifies the adjective *silent* to convey the manner (how) in which the class was silent. The adjective phrases then in turn modify the head noun *class*.
- Adverbs may modify determiners in a determiner phrase. An example of such a determiner phrase is *only four* in <u>*Only four*</u> *students signed up for the badminton tournament.* The adverb *only* premodifies the determiner *four* to emphasise this quantifier *four*. The determiner phrase *only four* then modifies the head noun *students* to form the noun phrase *Only four students*.
- Adverbs may modify sentences by conveying a speaker's or writer's opinion or stance. For example, the adverb *frankly* in <u>*Frankly*</u>, *I do not care,* modifies the speaker's or writer's stance expressed in the sentence *I do not care* to convey the honest stance taken on by the speaker/writer. Adverbs used this way are usually (not always) placed before the sentence to be modified. Other such adverbs include *fortunately, honestly, interestingly* and *luckily*.
- Adverbs may also be used to link sentences. For example, the adverb *consequently* links the sentences here – *Celia missed many tennis practice sessions. Consequently, she was not selected for the school tennis team.* This may also be written as *Celia missed many tennis practice sessions; consequently, she was not selected for the school tennis team* using the semi-colon to join the two related main (or independent) clauses. The adverb *consequently* links and creates a relationship of cause-and-effect between the two main clauses (or ideas).

In terms of distribution and positioning within a sentence, adverbs are quite mobile. Adverbs typically occur in three different positions – at the beginning of a sentence, in the middle of a sentence (after the subject, either before a verb or between the auxiliary and the main verb) and at the end of a sentence. The positioning of the adverbs depends on considerations like the type of adverbs, the clause structure and the need for emphasis. For example, adverbs of manner can appear in all three positions mentioned, as in the following:

<u>*Quickly*</u>, *Min ran to the playground.*

Min <u>quickly</u> ran to the playground.

Min ran to the playground <u>quickly</u>.

Adverbs of time can appear both at the beginning and the end of a sentence as in the following:

Hiro will see his daughter tomorrow.

Tomorrow, Hiro will see his daughter.

(Note: when adverbs of time appear in the front of a sentence, there is an emphasis on the adverb of time.)

It would be odd to have the adverb of time, *tomorrow*, appear in the middle of the sentence as in **Hiro will tomorrow see his daughter.*

Adverbs of place, however, tend to appear at the end of the sentence as in the following:

Anisya went outside.

While it is possible to have the adverb *outside* appear in front of the sentence as in, *Outside, Anisya went*, this is not very common. It is also not acceptable for this adverb to appear in the middle of the sentence as in **Anisya outside went.*

Where the adverb appears sometimes also depends on the structure of the clause. For example, if the clause has a direct object, the adverb will usually appear after the direct object – as in, *Eva ate the delicious cake quickly.* It is not wrong, though, for the adverb *quickly* to appear before the verb *ate*, as in *Eve quickly ate the delicious cake.* The preference, however, is for the adverb of manner to appear after the direct object in a clause with a direct object.

From the discussion above, you will note that there are no hard-and-fast rules about the distribution or position of adverbs in sentences. An adverb is one of the most mobile word classes in a sentence and its preferred position in a sentence depends on a variety of factors.

It is important to distinguish between adverbs/adverb phrases and adverbials. Adverbs and adverb phrases are forms that can play the functional role of adverbials in clauses. Adverbials answer the when, where, why and how questions of the main verb in a clause. Just like adverbs and adverb phrases, adverbials are mobile in clauses and sentences. Please do note, however, that adverbials can be of other forms, like noun phrases, preposition phrases and finite/non-finite clauses, and not just limited to adverbs and adverb phrases.

Determiners (Det)

Meaning

Words that are determiners determine both the reference (i.e., where the noun is) as well as the quantity of nouns. We can categorise determiners into five groups – (definite and indefinite) articles (for example, *a* and *the*), quantifiers (for example, *some, many, two, seventh*), demonstratives (for example, *this, these*), possessive determiners (for example, *my, his, their*) and interrogative determiners (for example, *which, what*).

Form

Some determiners are either singular or plural. For example, demonstratives like *that* indicate singular and *those* indicate plural. These determiners which are either singular or plural need to agree with the head noun in a noun phrase. This means that a singular head noun would entail the use of a singular determiner and a plural head noun would entail the use of a plural determiner (for example, *this cat* vs *these cats*). Some quantifiers like *few, many, little* and *much* which behave like determiners also must agree with countable or uncountable nouns. Nouns that can be counted (countable nouns) occur with quantifiers like *few* and *many* (for example, *many pencils*), and nouns that cannot be counted (uncountable nouns) occur with quantifiers like *little* and *much* (for example, *much sugar*).

Function

Determiners always occur before nouns and adjectives in noun phrases. An important point to note about determiners is that because the role of a determiner is to point to and modify a noun or nouns, the determiner cannot stand alone. The various roles of determiners are the following:

- Articles serve to determine nouns as having a definite or an indefinite reference. For example, if one says *I saw a cat in the store*, this is the first mention of this cat and this cat is not a specific cat that is known to the hearer. However, if one says, *I saw the cat in the store*, this would not be a first mention, and this cat would be a known, specific and identifiable animal to the hearer. The definite article *the* can also be used to refer to a general class of things, for example, in *The cat is a feline creature*, where the definite article *the* is not referring to a specific cat but making a generic reference to the general class of cats.
- Demonstrative determiners serve a deictic function – this means that demonstratives situate nouns within space or time in relation to the speaker/writer or hearer/reader. For example, in saying *These flowers are fresher than those flowers*, the demonstrative *these* is referring to the flowers closer to the speaker and the demonstrative *those* is referring to the flowers located further from the speaker. In saying, *I enjoyed myself this evening but had a horrible time that evening*, the use of the demonstratives *this* versus *that* contrasts the time in relation to the moment this sentence was spoken by the speaker.
- Possessive determiners signal possession of a particular noun or nouns. For example, the determiner *his* in the noun phrase *his books* signals that the books belong to the male person indicated by *his*. The use of the possessive suffix *–'s* in *John's* also results in *John's* acting as a possessive determiner where *John's books* is similar to *his books* (where *his* is a possessive determiner).

- Quantifiers serve to quantify nouns. Examples of these quantifiers include *few, many, little, much, some, several, each, every* and cardinal (for example, *three, one hundred*) and ordinal (for example, *third, hundredth*) numbers.
- Interrogative determiners function to question the reference of a noun or nouns. Examples of interrogative determiners include *which, what* and *whose*. For example, in *Whose bag is this?*, *whose* is an interrogative determiner questioning the reference of the noun. A possible answer could be *Meiling's bag*, where *Meiling's* would be a possessive determiner.

Pronouns (Pron)

Meaning

Words that are pronouns are used in place of nouns and noun phrases. Pronouns are largely used to avoid the repetition of nouns and noun phrases, to create conciseness in expressions. There are various types of pronouns expressing different meanings:

- Personal pronouns identify speakers, addressees and others in the act of communication. Examples of personal pronouns are *I, you, it, he, him, them* and *we*.
- Possessive pronouns convey ownership. Examples of possessive pronouns are *mine, yours, its, hers, theirs* and *ours*.
- Reflexive pronouns point to a noun or a pronoun that appears somewhere else in a clause. Examples of reflexive pronouns are *myself, yourself, itself, herself, themselves* and *ourselves*.
- Reciprocal pronouns convey a two-way relationship. These pronouns are *each other* and *one another*.
- Demonstrative pronouns signal a contrast between 'near' and 'far' with respect to the speaker. Examples of demonstrative pronouns are *this* and *those*.
- Relative pronouns link a relative clause to the head noun of a noun phrase. Examples of relative pronouns are *who, which, that* and *whose*.
- Interrogative pronouns are used to ask questions about other nouns and noun phrases. Examples of interrogative pronouns are *what, who* and *which*.
- Indefinite pronouns indicate a less specific meaning than the pronouns mentioned above and refer to people or things in a general way. Examples of indefinite pronouns are *someone, something, anyone, anybody* and *everybody*.

Form

The forms of pronouns depend on person, gender, number and case.

- Person refers to whether the pronouns are in the first, second or third persons, and these are based on the distance from the speaker. For example,

I, a first-person pronoun refers to the speaker, *you*, a second person refers to the listener, and *he*, a third person pronoun, refers to another distanced from the speaker.
- Number refers to whether the pronouns are singular or plural. For example, *herself* is a singular reflexive pronoun and *themselves* is a plural reflexive pronoun. Do note that the second person pronoun *you* and the possessive pronoun *yours* may be either singular or plural.
- Gender refers to whether the pronouns are male (for example, *he*), female (for example, *her*s) or sex-neutral (for example, *it*).
- Case refers to the function or position the pronouns have in a sentence. For example, the first-person pronoun in the subject position is *I* as in *I saw the man* and the first person pronoun in the object position is *me* as in *The man saw me*).

The forms of the pronoun to use also depend on whether the noun that the pronoun is standing in for is a person, animal or thing. For example, the relative pronoun *who* will be used if the head noun that the pronoun is referring to is a person as in the noun phrase *The lady who is wearing a pink shirt*, while the relative pronoun *which* will be used if the head noun that the pronoun is referring to is a thing as in the noun phrase *The book which I had read*.

Function

Pronouns can stand alone and need not be attached to another noun. It is important to note here that there is a difference between pronouns and determiners. As mentioned, a pronoun stands in for a noun or a noun phrase, and so can stand alone. A determiner, on the other hand, must be accompanied by a noun and as such, cannot stand alone. Some pronouns and determiners share the same form, and so it is important to pay attention to the distribution and function of these words in the context of a sentence to determine if these words are behaving as pronouns or determiners. For example, the words *his* and *her* may either function as a possessive pronoun or a possessive determiner depending on where and how these words are used in a phrase or sentence. In the example *His car broke down*, *his* is used as a possessive determiner as it pre-modifies the noun *car* and cannot stand alone in this context. In the example *This car is his*, *his* is used as a possessive pronoun as *his* in fact stands in for the noun phrase *his car*. In terms of functional roles pronouns play in the context of a sentence, depending on where they occur in a sentence, pronouns can play the roles of subjects, objects or complements.

Prepositions (Prep)

Meaning

Words that are prepositions express relationships between two parts of a sentence. The part that comes after the preposition is the complement of the preposition and this complement is a noun, pronoun, noun phrase or clause that acts like a noun. The part before the preposition is a noun or a noun phrase, an adjective or an adjective phrase or a verb or a verb phrase. Prepositions express various relationships such as those of:

- space – For example, the preposition *under* in *I found the bracelet under the bed* signals where *the bracelet* (noun phrase) is in relation to *the bed* (noun phrase). Other prepositions that express relationships of space include *in, on, to, over, out of, across, along* and *around*.
- time – For example, the preposition *during* in *The audience is silent during the performance* signals when the audience is *silent* (adjective or adjective phrase) in relation to *the performance* (noun phrase). Other prepositions that express relationships of time include *at, until, on, over* and *for*. You will notice that some prepositions like *in, on* and *over* may appear both as spatial and temporal prepositions depending on the contexts in which they are used.
- cause – For example, the preposition *because of* in *Rina fell because of the wet floor* signals that the reason Rina *fell* (verb or verb phrase) is due to *the wet floor* (noun phrase). Other prepositions that express relationships of cause like reason, purpose and motive are *for, due to* and *on account of*.
- means – For example, the preposition *by* in *Tina made the lantern by using recycled paper* signals that the manner in which *the lantern* (noun phrase) was made was *using recycled paper* (*-ing* clause behaving as a noun). Examples of other prepositions that express relationships of means like manner and instrument are *like, as, with* and *from*.
- accompaniment – For example, the preposition *with* in *Wenhua attended the concert with his best friend* signals that Wenhua attended *the concert* (noun phrase) in the company of *his best friend* (noun phrase). Another example of a preposition that expresses a relationship of accompaniment is *without*.
- concession – For example, the preposition *in spite of* in *The Pereiras are not proud in spite of their success* signals that the Pereiras are not *proud* (adjective or adjective phrase) although they have *their success* (noun phrase) – this is in contrast to the usual expectation that successful people are proud in nature. Other examples of prepositions that express relationships of concession are *despite* and *notwithstanding*.

Form

There are different forms of prepositions and these include single-word and multi-word prepositions. Examples of single-word prepositions are *in, on, over, below* and *past*. Examples of multi-word prepositions are *next to, out of, in front of, in spite of* and *in order to*.

Function

As mentioned earlier, prepositions always come before (hence *pre*position) complements which take the form of a noun, pronoun, noun phrase or a clause which acts like a noun. A preposition thus functions to relate its complement to another unit such as a noun or a noun phrase, an adjective or an adjective phrase or a verb or a verb phrase. The preposition and the complement together form a preposition phrase. A preposition phrase may function as the postmodifier to a head noun in a noun phrase, a subject, an indirect object, a complement or an adverbial in a sentence depending on the context.

Conjunctions (Conj)

Meaning

Words that are conjunctions connect like words or groups of words. Conjunctions (underlined here) join words of the same word class (for example, adjective + adjective as in *rich but humble*) and groups of words like similar phrases (for example, noun phrase + noun phrase as in *buttery scones and hot tea*) and clauses (for example, *He will buy himself a car when he has saved enough money*). It is important that conjunctions link words, phrases, clauses and sentences that are similar in meaning and form. For example, this sentence *John drank some juice and was eating some cake* sounds odd because the verb phrases in the conjoined clauses do not take the same form – *drank* is in the simple past and *was eating* is in the past progressive. Conjunctions link ideas and contribute to the flow and cohesiveness of a piece of text.

Conjunctions can largely be categorised into two kinds – coordinating conjunctions and subordinating conjunctions. Coordinating conjunctions connect parts of sentences that are grammatically equal, in other words, coordinating conjunctions connect ideas that are of equal importance. Typically, there are seven identified coordinating conjunctions, forming the acronym FANBOYS. These are *for, and, neither . . . nor* (including *either . . . or . . .*), *but, or, yet* and *so*. These coordinating conjunctions express different meanings. For example, *and* typically conveys the meaning of addition of two parts, and *but* conveys the meaning of contrast between two parts.

There are many more subordinating conjunctions than coordinating conjunctions. For this reason, it is not possible to provide an acronym that might capture a comprehensive list of subordinating conjunctions. Some teachers use the acronym I SAW A WABUB to remind students of the main subordinating conjunctions – I (*if*) S(*since*) A (*as*) W (*when*) A (*although*) W (*while*) A (*after*) B (*before*) U (*until*) B (*because*). Please do bear in mind though that this acronym does not capture the comprehensive list of subordinating conjunctions. Subordinating conjunctions are used to signal the relationship between ideas or clauses that are not grammatically equal. They are used to join a main clause that conveys the main idea in a sentence, with a subordinate clause that conveys the supporting idea of the main clause in a sentence. For example, in the sentence *Habibah fled the scene when she heard footsteps*, the subordinate clause *when she heard footsteps* starting with the subordinating conjunction *when* provides the supporting idea to the main clause *Habibah fled the scene*, indicating that the main event happened at the time Habibah heard the footsteps. Do take note that the main clause or the main idea can stand alone here – *Habibah fled the scene* – but the subordinate clause or supporting idea cannot stand alone – **When she heard the footsteps*. In this way, the subordinating conjunction also creates a relationship between the main clause and the subordinate clause. The kind of relationship created depends on the choice of the subordinating conjunction used. For example, the use of *when* in this example signals that the main clause and the subordinate clause are related temporally. However, if another subordinating conjunction *because* is used to create the subordinate clause – *because she heard footsteps* – the relationship between the main clause and the subordinate clause will be one of causation.

Form

There are three forms of conjunctions. Some are single conjunctions like *and, yet, while* and *since*, some are complex conjunctions of more than a single word like *so that, in order that* and *even though*, and some conjunctions come in pairs. These conjunctions that come in pairs are known as correlative conjunctions. Examples of correlative conjunctions include *either . . . or . . .*, *neither . . . nor . . .* and *not only . . . but also . . . .*

Function

As mentioned earlier, conjunctions serve to conjoin similar parts of sentences – words, phrases, clauses and sentences. When conjunctions join clauses, depending on the type of conjunctions used, different types of sentences are formed. When coordinating conjunctions are used to join clauses, compound sentences are created. In compound sentences, the clauses joined are grammatically equal in status. For example, in the compound sentence, *Shi Ling did not study for her history paper, yet she passed it with flying colours*, both the clauses (ideas) *Shi Ling did not study for her history paper* and *She passed it with flying colours* are of equal importance.

When subordinating conjunctions are used to join clauses, complex sentences result. In complex sentences, a relationship is created between a main clause and one or more subordinate clauses, meaning that a relationship is formed between grammatically unequal clauses – the main clause carries the main idea and the subordinate clause carries the supporting idea. For example, in the complex sentence, *Shi Ling passed her history paper with flying colours although she did not study for it*, the main clause, *Shi Ling passed her history paper with flying colours*, carries the main idea while the subordinate clause *although she did not study for it*, only supports this main idea, giving additional information.

When both coordinating and subordinating conjunctions are used to join clauses, a compound-complex sentence results. In compound-complex sentences, the coordinating conjunctions join main clauses and the subordi nating conjunctions join main and subordinate clauses. For example, in the compound-complex sentence *Shi Ling passed her history paper with flying colours **and** (she) achieved the top place in class **although** she did not study for the paper*, the main clauses are joined with the coordinating conjunction *and* and the subordinate (or supporting) clause is joined through the use of the subordinating conjunction *although*.

In terms of function, the subordinate clauses as used in the complex and compound-complex sentences here play the role of adverbial.

As mentioned earlier, when learning a new word, apart from knowing its meaning, it is also important to know the possible word class(es) it belongs to so that we can use the word correctly in the context of phrases and sentences, to create meaning. How might being able to label or classify the word classes of words as used in a text help with the understanding of how language is used? Labelling helps to create awareness of how the text was put together, given that a text is weaved starting from words, which form phrases, then clauses, and then sentences. As mentioned earlier, words are the building blocks of a text. Having the metalanguage or the vocabulary to analyse and discuss how a text has been put together is empowering for both teachers and learners.

To understand how a text has been meaningfully put together using words from various word classes, as mentioned in Chapter 1, let's take a look at an excerpt from the introductory chapter, 'The Fall', from the book *Where's Grandma?*

Words and Word Classes as Meaning Making in Texts

The unanalysed excerpt is presented first before the analysed excerpt is presented. The words in the excerpt are analysed according to the distinctive properties of the word classes presented in terms of meaning, form and function. You can try analysing the excerpt in terms of word class on your own first before referring to the analysed excerpt.

EXCERPT 2.1

> *Thin and tall, Grandma walked slowly but steadily to the door. I held her arm as we walked towards the lift and kept the door open as Grandma tottered inside.*

EXCERPT 2.1 (ANALYSED ACCORDING TO WORD CLASS)

> ^{Adj}*Thin* ^{Conj}*and* ^{Adj}*tall,* ^{N}*Grandma* ^{V}*walked* ^{Adv}*slowly* ^{Conj}*but* ^{Adv}*steadily* ^{Prep}*to* ^{Det}*the* ^{N}*door.* ^{Pron}*I* ^{V}*held* ^{Det}*her* ^{N}*arm* ^{Conj}*as* ^{Pron}*we* ^{V}*walked* ^{Prep}*towards* ^{Det}*the* ^{N}*lift* ^{Conj}*and* ^{V}*kept* ^{Det}*the* ^{N}*door* ^{Adv}*open* ^{Conj}*as* ^{N}*Grandma* ^{V}*tottered* ^{Adv}*inside.*

Let's use the metalanguage that we now have for word classes to discuss this excerpt in terms of how the writer has put these words together to create meaning. From the analysis, it is clear that this short excerpt is rich in terms of the use of a variety of words from the word classes introduced above. In this excerpt from Chapter 1 of the book, the author has weaved together words from all the word classes to introduce the main characters of this narrative, who are Grandma and Luke (do note that the author writes as Luke, using the first person), and to establish the relationship between them.

To describe Grandma, the author uses adjectives, adverbs and verbs. The author uses these adjectives, adverbs and verbs effectively by interestingly employing the use of conjunctions. Using conjunctions which link similar parts of a sentence like similar words and phrases, the author connects adjectives in *Thin and tall* (modifying the noun phrase *Grandma* to describe how she looked like) and adverbs in *slowly but steadily* (modifying the verb *walked* to describe how Grandma walked) to portray an image of Grandma as quite frail. The author could have simply chosen to use one adjective and one adverb respectively, but he chose to employ the use of coordinating conjunctions, *and* and *but* to add more description to Grandma. The author also uses the conjunction *and* to connect the clauses *walked towards the lift* and *kept the door open* to add information to create a more vivid image of the scene. In addition, the author uses the subordinating conjunction *as* twice in the sentence *I held her arm as we walked towards the lift and kept the door open as Grandma tottered inside*. In this short paragraph, the author has purposefully used conjunctions to not only add more descriptions and information but has also created rhythm to the paragraph with this patterned use of the conjunctions.

Such an analysis and discussion of how the author has used words from various word classes to write, express meaning and add flow to the text would not have been possible without an awareness or understanding of word classes.

Having knowledge of word classes can also help one to decipher or guess the meaning of unfamiliar words when reading a piece of text. For example, some may be unfamiliar with the word *tottered* in the text. When there is a lack of understanding of meaning, one can turn to the form and function of the various word classes to guess the possible word class an unfamiliar word may belong to. In terms of form, the word *tottered* seems to carry the -*ed* suffix, which could possibly be the past tense -*ed* suffix of a verb. Given that this excerpt is written in the past tense, this suffix could indeed be the past tense suffix. In terms of function, the word *tottered* appears after the subject *Grandma* – and as we have learned, verbs tend to occur after the subject. That *tottered* might be a verb, is further strengthened by the fact that this word is followed by the adverb of place, *outside*. Adverbs typically modify verbs. If we look at patterns, we can also note similarity in clause structure with the use of the conjunction *and* here – <u>*as we walked towards the lift*</u> and *kept the door open* <u>*as Grandma tottered inside*</u> – suggesting that the words following the subordinating conjunction *as* and the subjects *we* and *Grandma* respectively are words that express actions, that is, verbs (like the known verb *walked*). In this way, drawing on knowledge of the form and function of word classes, one can decipher the word class an unfamiliar word belongs to, and in turn, then, make an intelligent guess on the possible meaning of the unfamiliar word based on the context of a piece of text. Here, one could possibly guess that the word *tottered* is a verb, and perhaps a word expressing movement (like the verb *walked*). Being able to guess the word class of an unfamiliar word within a text could then help with understanding the possible role the word plays within the text, and in turn, help with narrowing down the possible meanings of the word, leading to a better comprehension of the text.

Exploring Words and Word Class with 13- and 14-Year-Olds

In this section, we will explore how Alvin taught the concept of word class to three classes of 13- and 14-year-olds. Alvin is an experienced English teacher who has been teaching since he became qualified. At the point of the project, he was teaching at an all-girls independent school known for attracting highly successful students (independent schools are secondary schools in Singapore where the Ministry of Education allows them the flexibility to set their own fees and develop their academic and non-academic curricula). One of the challenges Alvin faced was that, while his students were high readiness learners, they came from different primary schools with varying levels of grammar knowledge.

Some students were good at memorising and could write and speak fluently, but Alvin believed that it was important for them to understand that grammar forms the basis of good writing. Alvin saw grammar, reading and writing as a natural progression, where engaging students in reading and writing activities reinforced their understanding of grammar, including its meaning, form and function. Reading, in particular, allowed students to apply their knowledge of word classes to understand unfamiliar words. Alvin chose to focus on word classes as he felt this would create an awareness in students of the various word possibilities and how words can behave in context for character development in writing these biographies.

The purpose of Alvin's lessons on word classes was primarily centred on guiding students towards crafting effective biographies. To achieve this, he strategically curated authentic texts that would help his learners with this objective. By analysing these texts, his students could appreciate their relevance and appropriateness in the context of biographical writing. Each authentic text served as a model for character description, fostering an understanding of how word classes could be used to portray individuals within biographies. Through engaging activities, students honed their skills in character depiction, laying the groundwork for effectively narrating life stories. Ultimately, Alvin's lessons aimed to cultivate a keen awareness of linguistic nuances, empowering his students to articulate their biographies with greater depth and clarity.

The lesson started off with a task aimed to trigger prior knowledge of the concept of word classes. This was adapted from a lesson on word classes which he had taught previously but not in a contextualised manner (Table 2.1).

Table 2.1 Word classes.

Word class	Definition	Underline the word(s) in each sentence functioning as the word class
Nouns	Used to name things, ideas, people, places, and events.	• She is a <u>student</u>. • She plays the <u>piano</u>. • She was in <u>school</u>. • She attended a <u>concert</u>. • She longs for <u>freedom</u>.
Verbs	Used to talk about actions or to describe a state of things.	• She <u>is</u> a student. • She <u>plays</u> the piano. • She <u>became</u> a music conductor. • She <u>thinks</u> too much.
Adjectives	Used to describe how things, people, or places look or feel.	• She drives a <u>blue</u> car. • She is <u>pretty</u>. • She was a <u>diligent</u> student. • The road was <u>busy</u>.
Adverbs	Used to describe the circumstances in which the event took place, telling us the how, when, and where of an action or state.	• She walked <u>hurriedly</u> to her next class. • She <u>often</u> plays the piano in the evening. • <u>Please</u> wait here for him. • He <u>eventually</u> left.
Pronouns	Used in place of nouns and may 'stand in' for a person, place, thing, or idea.	• The lady is sad. <u>She</u> has failed the test. • The brake is faulty. <u>It</u> must be replaced. • The fireman is searching for the elderly woman. <u>He</u> has been looking for <u>her</u> for ten minutes.
Determiners	Used to clarify what the noun refers to–they determine both the reference as well as the quantity.	• Lilian has <u>a</u> dog. She loves <u>the</u> dog! • <u>Four</u> persons have arrived. • I like <u>this</u> sofa, not <u>that</u> sofa. • <u>Many</u> people are in his house.
Prepositions	Used to relate nouns, pronouns, or noun phrases to one another, usually in space or time–they can be used to talk about where something comes from, what position something is in relation to another, and what time something is in relation to another event.	• The pen is <u>on</u> the desk. • I shall meet you <u>after</u> the lesson. • She disappeared <u>during</u> the lecture. • The car has gone <u>round</u> the bend.
Conjunctions	Used to join similar words or groups of words.	• The girl <u>and</u> her siblings are in the garden. • <u>Either</u> Peter <u>or</u> Parker did it. • I am exhausted <u>but</u> thankful.

Contents adapted from Alsagoff (2008)

This was followed by another task where Alvin introduced an authentic text of Asian origin. The novel he chose was *Adrift: My Childhood in Colonial Singapore* by David T.K. Wong who recounts the journey of the protagonist Tzi Ki, a young boy separated from his mother and raised by his grandmother in Singapore in 1935. *Adrift* is the first of several novels that Wong wrote. It is a family memoir that describes Tzi Ki's tumultuous upbringing, spanning his early years in Canton, his childhood in Singapore within complex extended families, and his teenage years in Perth having escaped the Japanese Occupation of Singapore. The following were two interconnected activities adapted from an excerpt from the novel that described one of Tzi Ki's two grandmothers, Ah Mah (Chinese for grandmother). The first activity required students to engage with both textual notes and an accompanying visual representation of Ah Mah. This preliminary task was designed to serve as a conceptual scaffold for the ensuing activity.

	Interview Notes
Photograph of Ah Mah and David T.K. Wong as a young boy	• That's my grandmother in the photo; my dad's mom • I had 4 grandparents, but this one I remember the most • I called her Ah Mah in Cantonese since young • Everyone, family and servants, naturally respected her; she had this presence • Her hair was always held up this way using pow fa, something like gel but made from camphor wood and hot water, maybe because of the grey hair • She had this smell, it made me feel safe; no one else had this smell

Text adapted from *Adrift: My Childhood in Colonial Singapore* by David T.K. Wong

Following up on this first activity, Alvin designed an interesting activity involving carefully placed nonsense words from an excerpt. Students were tasked to replace the selected nonsense words with ones that were familiar to them. This creative activity focused on the knowledge of form and function of word class. The nonsense words compelled Alvin's students to put 'meaning' aside, while relying on their knowledge of the form (shape of the word) and function (their distribution within context – specifically in relation to neighbouring words to decipher the word class of the word). This prompted his students to be more cognisant of the shape of a word (form) and the position of a word within a sentence (function). By engaging in this activity, Alvin's students had the opportunity to apply their understanding of word classes in a practical manner. They had to categorise the nonsense words into noun, verb, adjective or adverb classes, strengthening their grasp of word class concepts.

Alvin's Nonsense Words activity:

Of my four grandparents, the one who has (1) <u>melacated</u> most deeply lodged in my memory is my paternal grandmother. I learnt at an early stage to address her as Ah Mah, in the Cantonese fashion. She was a (2) <u>malified</u> woman, with a (3) <u>melantly</u> bearing. Family members as well as servants deferred (4) <u>milously</u> to her. She wore her hair in a (5) <u>merage</u>. The whole arrangement was slicked down using a once-popular gel-like preparation known as pow fa, made from camphor wood in hot water. The hair (6) <u>merained</u> a few strands of grey which I think she tried to (7) <u>mecent</u>. From a very early age, I had noted that a distinctive bodily fragrance was associated with her presence. It seemed to bring a feeling of comfort and (8) <u>meculity</u> which I could not find with anyone else, not even with my own mother.

Text adapted from *Adrift: My Childhood in Colonial Singapore* by David T.K. Wong

Alvin then posed the following reflection questions for his students to ponder:

- Was it easy or challenging to identify the word class that each underlined word belongs to? Why?
- What clues or guidelines did we use to decide on the word class that each underlined word belongs to?
- How has knowing the forms and functions of the various word classes helped us with comprehending a text (even if it contains unfamiliar words)?

The activity using nonsense words within the provided text can be highly beneficial for reinforcing the concept of word class, supporting the teaching of reading, and facilitating the teaching of writing.

Reinforcing Word Class

By replacing selected words in the authentic text with nonsense words, students are required to focus on the heuristics of form and function of words to determine the word classes of the nonsense words. This activity prompts them to analyse the function and form of each word, allowing for a deeper understanding of how word classes influence sentence meaning.

Let's look at the following two sentences:

Family members as well as servants deferred (4) <u>milously</u> to her. She wore her hair in a (5) <u>merage</u>.

To determine the word classes of the nonsense words *milously* and *merage*, students would need to consider the structure or form of these words and the co-text of these words (the neighbouring words). Through analysis, students would guess that *milously* is possibly an adverb and *merage* is possibly a noun.

In terms of form, the nonsense word *milously* takes on the suffix *-ly*, typical of other adverbs and in terms of function, *milously* occurs after the verb *deferred* – a common position of adverbs to modify verbs. As for the nonsense word *merage*, in terms of function, it appears after the determiner *a*. A determiner always occurs with a noun as the function of a determiner is to point to a noun. As there are no other words after the determiner *a* in this example, *merage* must be a noun.

Supporting the Teaching of Reading

Integrating nonsense words within the authentic text presents a challenge for students during the reading process. They must actively engage with the text, relying on their comprehension skills and knowledge of word classes to make sense of the content. By analysing the possible word classes of these nonsensical words based on their form and function, students can better engage with the text. Identifying the likely word classes of these nonsense words, even without understanding their meanings, supports students in comprehending the text. This ability can also extend to comprehending other texts containing unfamiliar words. Hence, highlighting the significance of such skills when encountering unknown words strengthens students' reading comprehension skills. Alvin in his interview commented that the value-add in this lesson is that when students analyse nonsense words, they are forced to draw on their knowledge of form and function of words.

For example, in the sentence *The hair (6) merained a few strands of grey which I think she tried to (7) mecent*, students would need to analyse structure of the words and the co-text of the words to comprehend the possible meaning of the nonsense words *merained* and *mecent*. Through analysis, students could infer that *merained* refers to the presence of strands of grey hair, while *mecent* could suggest an attempt to hide or conceal the grey strands.

Students would guess that the nonsense word *merained* is a verb, denoted by the past tense *-ed* suffix (FORM). In terms of distribution, this word appears between two noun phrases, *The hair* and *a few strands of grey hair which I think she tried to disguise*, a typical position of verbs to describe an action between two noun phrases (FUNCTION).

Similarly, students would guess that *mecent* is also a verb, representing the base form following a *to*-infinitive (FORM). In terms of its distribution, *mecent* is part of a verb chain containing the catenative verb *tried* which is followed by the *to*-infinitive + base form structure (for example, 'tried to eat', 'tried to sing', 'tried to sleep'). Other catenative verbs, like 'want', follow a similar pattern, such as 'want to eat' (FUNCTION).

Facilitating the Teaching of Writing

The inclusion of nonsense words within the authentic text encourages students to enhance their writing skills. They are prompted to replace nonsense words with appropriate real words while maintaining grammatical accuracy and cohesion within the sentence structure and hence, the text provides opportunities for students to practise vocabulary expansion, sentence construction, and grammar usage, fostering their overall writing proficiency. During his interview, Alvin remarked that while reviewing the drafts, he was pleased to observe a notable shift in storytelling style. He noticed that many of his students had transitioned from telling to showing, demonstrating a greater activity in their utilisation of different word classes. This change allowed them to highlight more of the subject's qualities.

For example, in the sentence *It seemed to bring a feeling of comfort and (8) meculity which I could not find with anyone else, not even with my own mother*, students would need to analyse the form and function of the nonsense word *meculity* and choose appropriate real words to replace this nonsense word. Through analysis, students would identify the need for a noun that conveys a sense of tenderness or kindness, and they might choose a word like 'gentleness' or 'affection' to maintain the coherence and meaning of the sentence.

According to Alvin, by engaging with the text and analysing the role of nonsense words, his students developed a deeper understanding of word classes, improved their reading comprehension abilities, and enhanced their writing skills. He described this activity as combining the aspects of analysis, interpretation, and application, making it a valuable tool for reinforcing grammar concepts while simultaneously supporting both reading and writing development.

In the interview, Alvin expressed his perspective on theoretical knowledge, particularly in grammar, and its relevance to highly skilled writers. He stated, 'For the very good, I'm talking about the really good ones . . . it may not have offered so much to this kind of students.' However, he believed that theoretical knowledge contributed to sharpening their awareness, adding, 'It just made them even more aware. It sharpened their awareness even more.' Alvin highlighted the importance of theoretical knowledge for students with natural writing talent but lacking a solid grammatical foundation. He explained, 'They may just naturally be able to write well . . . but they may not have had the theoretical foundation with regard to grammar as form, meaning and function.' According to Alvin's observations, theoretical knowledge enhanced awareness and provided a grammatical foundation for those gifted in writing.

In discussing word classes as a tool for making meaning in reading, Alvin emphasised its importance in providing readers with the necessary tools to decipher text effectively. He noted that understanding word classes in terms of form and function, and without relying on meaning alone enables readers to make more informed interpretations. Alvin highlighted how this understanding allows readers to intelligently guess the meaning of words, discerning whether they denote actions, describe other actions, function as nouns, or describe other nouns. He explained that this comprehension aids in making more precise interpretations. Transitioning to writing, Alvin underscored how awareness of word classes prompted his students to consider various options for creating and conveying meaning accurately. He pointed out that knowing the different types of word classes and how they interacted within a sentence could encourage writers to carefully select words to convey nuanced meanings with more precision. Alvin's approach to teaching word classes and grammar as a meaning-making resource was both practical and effective. The inclusion of the nonsense words activity proved valuable for reinforcing word class concepts, supporting reading comprehension, facilitating writing skills and more importantly, engaging his very bright students. His novel approach went beyond technical knowledge, offering students a hands-on experience that, we believe, further enhanced their understanding of grammar. Alvin's take on word classes and his carefully crafted activities not only addresses the challenges of varying levels of grammar knowledge but also emphasises the importance of a firm grammatical foundation for all learners, regardless of their natural writing talent. And as mentioned before, having the metalanguage to explain how a text comes together is empowering for both teachers and students.

Extract Used in Chapter 2

The following is the extract from the chapter 'My Grandparents', in *Adrift: My Childhood in Colonial Singapore*, written by David T.K. Wong.

Of my four grandparents, the one who has remained most deeply lodged in my memory is my paternal grandmother. She had taken care of me since my birth and I had her company, through thick and thin, for far longer than with any of the other three. From a very early age, I had noted that a distinctive bodily fragrance was associated with her presence. Thus long before I could even articulate her name, I had this means of identifying with her. I had no idea whether the smell was inherent in her person or whether it came from some perfume she wore. All I knew was that I liked it. It seemed to bring a feeling of comfort and security which I could not find with anyone else, not even with my own mother. That distinctive fragrance signalled her approach even before she came into view.

I learnt at an early stage to address her as Ah Mah, in the Cantonese fashion. She was a dignified woman, with a matronly bearing and wore her hair in a chignon. The hair contained a few strands of grey which I think she tried to disguise. The whole arrangement was slicked down using a once-popular gellike preparation known as 'pow fa', made from soaking shavings of camphor wood in hot water. She was already in her mid-fifties when I came into the world.

Another feature of hers I soon discovered was that she invariably wore on her right wrist a bracelet of translucent green jade. That cool ring of stone my infant fingers soon discovered provided another means by which to identify her. Sometimes she would wear a pair of matching earrings in the shape of small jade balls. She looked the perfect picture of a benign and self-assured matriarch. Family members as well as servants deferred automatically to her.

References

Alsagoff, L. (2008). *A Visual Grammar of English*. Pearson Education Asia.

Alsagoff, L. (2023). *A Visual Guide to English Grammar*. Marshall Cavendish International (Asia).

Halliday, M.A.K. & Matthiessen, C.M.I.M (2004). *An Introduction to Functional Grammar* (3rd ed.). Routledge. https://doi.org/10.4324/9780203783771

Wong, D.T.K. (2015). *Adrift: My Childhood in Colonial Singapore*. Epigram Books.

3 Nouns and Noun Phrases

From Words to Phrases

From word classes, let's now move on to phrases. Phrases are groups of words that come together to form constituents of clauses and sentences. Phrases are labelled according to the word class of the head or the most important word the phrase is built or structured around. For example, in the phrase *very talkative*, the head or the most important word anchoring the phrase is the adjective *talkative*. The adverb *very* is modifying the adjective *talkative*. As such, the phrase *very talkative* is labelled as an adjective phrase.

Let's consider another group of words coming together to form a phrase – *the very talkative girl*. Here, the head or most important word of this phrase is *girl* as the phrase is essentially about the girl. The word *girl* is a noun. Hence, the phrase is labelled as a noun phrase. You will notice that the adjective phrase *very talkative* is embedded within the noun phrase *the very talkative girl*. So, it is important to bear in mind that **a phrase may be embedded within another phrase**.

To explore this further, let's look at the phrase *in my class*. This phrase starts with a preposition *in*. When a phrase starts with a preposition, a preposition phrase is formed. As such, *in my class* is a preposition phrase with the head word being the preposition *in*. Let's return to our noun phrase *the very talkative girl*. This noun phrase may be extended by further modifying the head noun *girl* to *the very talkative girl in my class*, with the preposition phrase *in my class* adding more information to the noun *girl*. You will learn below that a head noun in a noun phrase may be postmodified by certain forms or structures, and one of these structures is a preposition phrase. As such, the phrase *the very talkative girl in my class* is still a noun phrase with the head of this phrase being the noun *girl*. The entire phrase *the very talkative girl in my class* is built around the head noun *girl*.

Before we move on to learn more about noun phrases, it is important to make another critical point about phrases which might seem contradictory to what we have discussed so far. Although we have defined a phrase as a group of words coming together to form a constituent, a phrase can be a single

DOI: 10.4324/9781003255963-3

word. This is because the term phrase refers to a level of analysis in grammar. In grammar, language is represented as being hierarchical in nature. We said earlier that words come together to form phrases which in turn form clauses and sentences, which ultimately leads to the production of texts. Instead of correlating this hierarchical nature of language to the number of words coming together at each 'level', we should consider each level as a different level of analysis. Let's consider our noun phrase *the very talkative girl in my class* within the context of a sentence as shown below:

The very talkative girl in my class received a bad scolding.

At the level of word class analysis, this sentence may be analysed as follows:

^{Det}*The* ^{Adv}*very* ^{Adj}*talkative* ^{N}*girl* ^{Prep}*in* ^{Det}*my* ^{N}*class* ^{V}*received* ^{Det}*a* ^{Adj}*bad* ^{N}*scolding*.

At the level of phrasal analysis, the sentence may be analysed as follows:

The noun phrase *the very talkative girl in my class* may be replaced by the pronoun *she*. In this case, the sentence will be analysed at phrasal level as below:

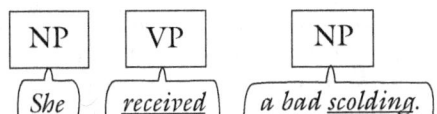

If the pronoun *she* is replaced by, for example, the name *Kyra*, *Kyra* will be analysed as a noun phrase at the phrasal level. As such, at the level of phrasal analysis, single words may be analysed as phrases.

You will notice from the analysis above that we have other phrases like verb phrases. The head of a verb phrase is the verb. In our example above, the verb phrase is *received*, comprising only of the main verb *received*. Verb phrases may also comprise auxiliary verbs like the verbs *be*, *has* and modal verbs like *will*, *should* and *must* (please refer to Chapter 4 for more on main and auxiliary verbs). For example, in the sentence *She will receive a bad scolding*, the verb phrase is *will receive*.

Now that we have a better understanding of phrases in general, let's discuss noun phrases specifically in detail.

A Noun Phrase

A noun phrase contains an obligatory **head** noun, and as such, is like a noun answering the 'who' and the 'what' questions in a clause. The noun phrase usually appears as the subject, object or complement of a clause, carrying the main information in texts. The noun phrases in a text usually tell us what the text is about.

The head noun may be modified within the noun phrase by other words, phrases and clauses. Modifiers that occur before the head noun are called **premodifiers** and those modifiers that occur after the head noun are called **postmodifiers**. The words 'head', 'modifiers', 'premodifiers' and 'postmodifiers' are functional terms that label the role these words play in a noun phrase. Premodifiers may be in the form of **determiners**, **adjectives** and other **nouns**, while postmodifiers may be in the form of **preposition phrases, relative clauses, non-finite clauses, postpositive adjectives/adjective phrases** and **postpositive adverbs/adverb phrases**. Using these (usually) optional premodifiers and postmodifiers allows us to create more complex noun phrases which add information to or describe the head noun.

Premodifiers in a Noun Phrase

To illustrate possible premodifiers and postmodifiers of a head noun in a noun phrase, let's start with the head noun, *clocks*. The head noun *clocks* is a plural noun and as such, it can stand alone in a sentence – for example:

Clocks are sold in that shop.

In this case, *clocks* is the head noun, and at the level of phrases, *clocks* is a noun phrase. However, if this head noun is *clock*, in its singular form, a determiner like *a* or *the* will be required – *The clock is sold in that shop* (do note also that the verb needs to be singular to agree with the singular head noun). Here, the noun phrase will be *the clock* – where the head noun *clock* is premodified by the determiner *the*. The head noun *clock* in the noun phrase *the clock* may be further premodified with the use of an adjective – for example, *The antique clock is sold in that shop*. The noun phrase now is expanded to *the antique clock*. You will note that the noun phrase becomes ungrammatical if the positions of the determiner and adjective are switched, like in **antique the clock*. As such, in terms of distribution, determiners come before adjectives in noun phrases. We can also have another noun premodify the head noun in a noun phrase – for example, *The antique metal clock* where *metal* refers to the material the clock is made of, hence a noun. When there is another noun premodifying the head noun in a noun phrase, the noun appears directly before the head noun. The noun phrase becomes ungrammatical or sounds odd otherwise, like in **the metal antique clock*. As such, by now, you would have come to realise that there is a certain order to the appearance of the premodifiers to a head noun in a noun phrase. The order of premodifiers is as follows:

determiner(s) > adjective(s) > noun(s) > **head noun**

To recap, the obligatory element in the noun phrase is the head noun and the rest of the premodifiers are optional (an exception being that when the head noun is a singular noun, the determiner is obligatory).

It is also essential to note that we can have more than one determiner, more than one adjective and more than one noun as premodifiers to a head noun. For example, the noun phrase *The expensive antique metal clock* has two different adjectives premodifying the head noun, *clock*. It is also possible for the head noun to be premodified by determiner phrases and adjective phrases as in the noun phrase *All the ten very expensive clocks* where the head noun *clocks* is premodified by the determiner phrase *all the ten* and the adjective phrase *very expensive*.

Using the examples of the noun phrase *The expensive antique metal clock* and *All the ten very expensive clocks*, the structure of a noun phrase containing premodifiers is as shown in Table 3.1.

Table 3.1 Structure of a noun phrase.

Determiner	Adjective	Noun	Head noun
The	expensive antique	metal	clock
All the ten	very expensive		clocks

Premodifiers add vivid and descriptive details to the noun phrase and they do so in a concise manner. For example, compare the noun phrase *the expensive antique metal clock* with premodifier adjectives and a premodifier noun, and the sentence *The clock is expensive and antique, and made of metal*. Both the noun phrase and the sentence express the same details about the noun *clock* but the expanded noun phrase *the expensive antique metal clock* expresses this in a more succinct manner.

Postmodifiers in a Noun Phrase

A head noun may also be postmodified as we saw in our earlier example *the very talkative girl in my class*. The preposition phrase *in my class* is a postmodifier modifying the head noun *girl*. Besides preposition phrases, there are several different forms or structures that can postmodify a head noun. The different structures are shown in Table 3.2 through various examples using *girl* or *girls* as the head nouns.

Table 3.2 Types of postmodifiers in a noun phrase.

Premodifier			Head noun	Postmodifier
Det	Adj	Noun		
The	very talkative		girl	in my class (preposition phrase as this postmodifier starts with a preposition *in*)

(*Continued*)

Table 3.2 (Continued)

Premodifier			Head noun	Postmodifier
Det	Adj	Noun		
Those			girls	<u>who</u> were scolded by the teacher
				(relative clause as this postmodifier starts with a relative pronoun *who*. Relative clauses can also start with relative adverbs like *where*.)
All the ten		school	girls	<u>standing</u> outside the classroom
				<u>shaken</u> by the incident
				<u>to perform</u> at the concert
				(non-finite clause as these postmodifier starts with non-finite verbs like the *-ing* participle, the *-ed/en* participle and the *to-infinitive* respectively)
That	radiant		girl	<u>aglow</u> in white
				(postpositive adjective/adjective phrase as this postmodifier starts with an adjective)
All the	extremely excited	dance	girls	<u>nearby</u>
				(postpositive adverb as this postmodifier starts with an adverb)

As pointed out in Table 3.2, the type of postmodifier may be identified by the first word that directly follows the head noun and starts the postmodifier.

Postmodifiers allow for more complex details to be introduced to the noun phrase as postmodifiers may be expressed through a variety of structures like preposition phrases, relative clauses, non-finite clauses, postpositive adjectives/adjective phrases and postpositive adverbs/adverb phrases.

As mentioned earlier, both premodifiers and postmodifiers are largely optional and function to describe or provide more information about the head noun. Given that these modifiers are optional, they are choices speakers or writers can make within the structure of the noun phrase to elaborate on the head noun or not. For example, it is evident from Tables 3.1 and 3.2 that not all the premodifier slots need to be filled. The choice of whether to include premodifiers or postmodifiers will depend on several factors like the purpose, audience, context or culture of the spoken or written text within which these noun phrases occur. This point will be illustrated through the analyses of the excerpts from the narrative *Where's Grandma?* in the next section.

Noun Phrases as Meaning Making in Texts

EXCERPT 3.1

> *Thin and tall, <u>Grandma</u> walked slowly but steadily to <u>the door</u>. <u>I</u> held <u>her arm</u> as <u>we</u> walked towards <u>the lift</u> and kept <u>the door</u> open as <u>Grandma</u> tottered inside.*
>
> *For <u>the past month</u>, <u>we</u> had not been to <u>the playground</u>. Instead, <u>we</u> went to <u>the neighbourhood park</u>. For <u>fifteen minutes</u> <u>every day</u>, <u>we</u> would stroll together so that <u>Grandma</u> could get <u>some fresh air</u> and <u>light exercise</u>.*

The noun phrases in Excerpt 3.1 (underlined) are analysed in detail in Table 3.3.

Table 3.3 Noun phrases in Excerpt 3.1.

Premodifier			Head noun	Postmodifier	Notes
Det	Adj	Noun			
			Grandma		repeated
the			door		repeated
			I		repeated
her			arm		
			we		repeated
the			lift		
the	past		month		
the			playground		
the		neighbourhood	park		
fifteen			minutes		
every			day		
some	fresh		air		
(some)	light		exercise		Determiner *some* ellipted in the second coordinated noun phrase to avoid repetition.

EXCERPT 3.2

> *<u>Grandma</u> was <u>a wonderful cook</u>. <u>She</u> made <u>lunch</u> for <u>both of us</u>. <u>I</u> could eat <u>two bowls of Grandma's delicious potato curry</u>. <u>I</u> will never forget <u>the smell of the curry</u> and <u>her tasty, chewy home-made ang ku kueh</u> – absolutely mouth-watering.*

Table 3.4 Noun phrases in Excerpt 3.2.

Premodifier			Head noun	Postmodifier	Notes
Det	Adj	Noun			
			Grandma		
a	wonderful		cook		
			she		
			lunch		
			both	of us (preposition phrase)	
			I		repeated
two			bowls	of Grandma's delicious potato curry (preposition phrase)	
the			smell	of the curry (preposition phrase)	
her	tasty, chewy home-made		*ang ku kueh* [a traditional Chinese pastry]		

EXCERPT 3.3

<u>Grandma</u> did not only take <u>me</u> to <u>the playground</u>. When <u>I</u> entered <u>Primary One</u>, <u>she</u> took <u>me</u> to <u>school</u> too. <u>Hand in hand</u>, <u>we</u> would walk to <u>school which was on the far side of the housing estate</u>. While <u>we</u> walked, <u>we</u> would talk about <u>the things we planned to do that day</u>. <u>I</u> liked <u>it</u> best when <u>she</u> took out <u>her special album of black and white photos</u> and told <u>me</u> <u>stories about her childhood in a small kampong in Penang</u>.

Table 3.5 Noun phrases in Excerpt 3.3.

Premodifier			Head noun	Postmodifier	Notes
Det	Adj	Noun			
			Grandma		
			me		repeated
the			playground		
			Primary One		

(*Continued*)

Nouns and Noun Phrases 41

Table 3.5 (Continued)

Premodifier			Head noun	Postmodifier	Notes
Det	Adj	Noun			
			she		repeated
			school		
			Hand	in hand (preposition phrase)	
			school	which was on the far side of the housing estate (relative clause)	
the			things	(that) we planned to do that day (relative clause with the relative pronoun ellipted)	
			it		
her	special		album	of black and white photos (preposition phrase)	
			me		
			stories	about her childhood in a small kampong in Penang (preposition phrase)	

Most of the head nouns in the noun phrases in *Where's Grandma?* are concrete nouns (for example, *lunch, bowls, ang ku kueh* and *school*), as opposed to abstract nouns. Proper and concrete nouns like Grandma (and Luke in other parts of the narrative) also appear frequently as head nouns to refer to the main characters in the narrative. Pronouns as head nouns are also used frequently to refer to the main characters of the narrative – the second-person pronoun *she* to refer to Grandma and the first-person pronoun *I* to refer to the grandson and the writer (named Luke in the narrative). The use of concrete nouns, proper nouns and personal pronouns as head nouns in this narrative is suitable for the target audience, which is that of young readers. The use of such head nouns allows young readers to follow the narrative easily, to visualise the setting and the characters in a concrete manner.

The noun phrases in *Where's Grandma?* are largely simple noun phrases made up of 'det + head noun' or 'det + adj + head noun' structures as can be seen in the analyses of the excerpts. This is especially so in the earlier parts of the narrative. The choice made by the author to largely use simple noun phrases in the narrative may be attributed, as mentioned before, to the target audience of the book, likely young readers. As the narrative progresses with more descriptions of Grandma and the surroundings, more complex noun phrases are used as seen in excerpts 3.2 and 3.3. However, it is important to note that most of the postmodifiers are of the preposition phrase structure, which is the postmodifier structure that is least complex, and used most by young writers. This choice once again may be attributable to the young audience this book is written for.

It is also important and interesting to note that the author chooses to develop noun phrases that are significant to the development of the narrative. For example, Grandma's *delicious potato curry* plays a significant role in the narrative. Grandma's talented ability to cook her signature potato curry dish pre-Alzheimer's disease and eventual loss of memory of how to cook this dish illustrates Grandma's deterioration of health. Later in the narrative, Luke joins Grandma in the kitchen to remind her how to cook her potato curry and this further develops the bond between grandmother and grandson. The author also chooses to expand on Grandma's album and stories. These also play a significant role in the narrative. When Grandma's Alzheimer's disease gets more serious, Grandma cannot recall where she had placed her album and gets angry when she cannot find it. When Luke finds it and hands it over to Grandma, Grandma gets so angry with Luke, thinking that he had taken it, and slaps him. The incident hurts Luke badly, physically and emotionally, as he realises that the disease was also making Grandma lose her personality. Grandma's deterioration of physical and mental health is contrasted with how Grandma was before – her previously healthy state of body and mind illustrated through how she used to walk Luke to *school which was on the far side of the housing estate*. The relative clause postmodifier *which was on the far side of the housing estate* used to elaborate on the head noun *school* is purposefully used by the author to emphasise that Grandma was strong before the onset of the disease.

The analyses above of the noun phrases highlights that choices may be made in the crafting of noun phrases to purposefully achieve the purposes of a text – be it to attend to the target audience of a text or to achieve the intent of a text (or narrative in this case).

As mentioned earlier, the noun phrases in the narrative *Where's Grandma?* are largely simple noun phrases. Let's now look at an excerpt from the novel *The Evergreen Tea House*, written by writer David T.K. Wong. This is a provocative and poignant novel written for a much older audience (compared to that of *Where's Grandma?*) that is set in Hong Kong during the twilight years of British rule. The following excerpt is from the chapter 'Dinner with Father' and richly describes the table laid out for the dinner that the main character in the novel, Chu Wing-sen, will have with his parents (the extract from which this excerpt is taken is found at the end of this chapter).

EXCERPT 3.4

> In front of <u>him</u>, <u>the table</u> was laid out with <u>all the formal accessories</u>. <u>Personalised ivory chopsticks with names engraved in red</u>. <u>Polished silver chopstick rests</u>. <u>Little square dishes of sauces and condiments</u>. <u>Embroidered linen napkins, immaculately starched and ironed</u>. <u>A centrepiece filled with fresh pink flowers whose name he did not know</u>. It was <u>a far cry from the simple dinners eaten with his mother in the small alcove in her private quarters</u>.

Table 3.6 Noun phrases in Excerpt 3.4.

Premodifier			Head noun	Postmodifier
Det	Adj	Noun		
			him	
the			table	
all the	formal		accessories	
	Personalised	ivory	chopsticks	with names engraved in red (preposition phrase)
	Polished	silver chopstick	rests	
	Little	square	dishes	of sauces and condiments (preposition phrase)
	Embroidered	linen	napkins	immaculately starched and ironed (non-finite clause)
A			centrepiece	filled with fresh pink flowers whose name he did not know (non-finite clause)
			It	
a	far		cry	from the simple dinners eaten with his mother in the small alcove in her private quarters (preposition phrase)

Interestingly, the excerpt which describes the table setting is largely written using just standalone noun phrases. The effect of using a string of noun phrases in this excerpt is that readers are drawn to focus on the accessories (the concrete head nouns) on the table. The complex noun phrases, with highly descriptive adjective and noun premodifiers and a variety of postmodifers, create very clear and vivid images of the accessories on the table, allowing readers to visualise the table setting. Given that the target audience of this text is that of older readers, the structures of the postmodifiers are also more varied and stylistic (for example, in the use of the non-finite clause in the noun phrase *embroidered linen napkins immaculately starched and ironed*) than what we saw in the *Where's Grandma?*'s excerpts which were largely only that of preposition phrases. We should also bear in mind that the author would have intentionally chosen to describe this ornate table setting in such vivid ways (using strings of complex noun phrases) so that this rare extravagant dinner with Chu Wing-sen's father is contrasted with the simple dinners that Chu Wing-sen usually has just with his mother. The author is then making grammatical choices in the use of his noun phrases in serving a purpose of the text here, that is, to contrast Chu Wing-sen's relationship with his father with that of his mother.

Exploring Noun Phrases with 11-Year-Olds

In this section, we will explore how Gajen introduced noun phrases to his class of 11-year-olds. Gajen is an experienced English teacher who has been teaching for many years. He has been teaching in his current school for a significant number of years and he holds a senior position in the English department. The school is a regular primary school situated in the Western part of the island and is situated in one of Singapore's many suburban public housing estates. According to Gajen, this current class of students are middle-readiness learners.

Gajen focused on introducing noun phrases to the students as part of the school's writing unit. He noticed that the students were not very strong at using descriptive language, especially in character descriptions. While his students had been exposed to noun phrases before, he had not taught them in the context of a literacy skill such as reading or writing. Gajen felt that if his students had more knowledge of expanding noun phrases, the descriptions in their writing would be so much richer.

Metalanguage has always been a challenge not only for students but also teachers. So it was with great interest that we learnt how Gajen tried to overcome this challenge here. As teaching grammar involved technical terms like premodifiers, determiners, quantifiers, and articles, Gajen had to create a chart to help his students understand these concepts better.

Despite the initial difficulties, the students gradually grasped the concept of premodifiers, which was easier for them compared to postmodifiers.

The lessons aimed to prepare the students for their writing assignment where they needed to describe characters using noun phrases. Gajen noted that some students performed well with premodifiers, while others struggled with postmodifiers. However, overall, he felt that the lesson was successful in helping students improve their descriptive writing skills, even though some weaker students still faced challenges. Gajen found that while there were varying levels of success among students, the activities were beneficial in preparing them for future writing assignments.

Gajen emphasised the critical role of teaching grammar, specifically focusing on noun phrases, within the context of writing. He underscored that it was not merely about rote memorisation but about fostering a deeper understanding and meaningful application of grammar concepts. Gajen also stressed the necessity of explicit instruction to ensure that his learners comprehended the nuances of noun phrases. For example, he had to revisit grammatical terms, such as determiners like *a*, *an* and *the*, in the noun phrase. While he acknowledged that grammar instruction was essential to equip students with the tools required for effective writing, he also admitted that it was challenging given the constraints of a limited class time frame as writing units are usually allotted a week to complete.

In discussing his teaching approach compared to the current practices at his school, Gajen underscored several key points. Firstly, he pointed out the absence of a specific approach within the units of work for engaging students in the identification of grammatical concepts within real-world texts. It must be noted that while the grammar components are embedded within the reading texts, teachers tend to teach these grammar items in isolation – which was probably what Gajen was alluding to. Gajen emphasised his belief in the significance of providing students with excerpts from well-crafted texts, a practice he integrated into his lesson on noun phrases to demonstrate the practical application of grammar in reading as well as writing. Additionally, he reflected on the timing of his lesson, suggesting that introducing it earlier in the academic year, when students faced less assessment pressure, could make it more engaging and effective. He stressed the importance of revisiting and reinforcing grammar concepts over time, allowing students to grasp their long-term value. Lastly, Gajen highlighted the significance of repetition in learning grammar terminology and metalanguage, expressing confidence that continued exposure to these concepts will ultimately benefit students, even if they initially encounter challenges.

The lesson had the following objectives. Learners would be able to:

1. identify noun phrases in sentences;
2. identify expanded noun phrases in paragraphs; and
3. create expanded noun phrases.

The end point of the lesson package was to have his students complete a short writing assignment that required them to clearly identify and effectively use noun phrases within their written pieces. Lesson flow:

- Prior knowledge of noun phrases was elicited.
- Pairs were asked to perform a visualisation activity comparing the two following paragraphs. In both instances, learners were asked to sketch the following, which was read by the teacher.

Paragraph 1: Clouds drifted lazily. A girl was at the park. The girl was carrying a bag. Her friend was waiting for her.

Paragraph 2: Many fluffy white clouds in the blue sky drifted lazily. A slim teenaged girl wearing a pale-yellow blouse and comfortable shorts was at the empty neighbourhood park which was just beside the playground. She was carrying a colourful plastic bag with many big juicy fruits. Her friend who was carrying a picnic mat was waiting for her.

Gajen's reason for putting his students through this activity was to raise awareness of the effectiveness of noun phrases in descriptive writing. He hoped that they would have a better understanding of the importance and application of expanded noun phrases for creating more focused and vivid descriptions in their writing.

Gajen's students were re-acquainted with the structure of the noun phrase concept. He elucidated this by using an illustration featuring definitions and examples to elaborate (Figure 3.1). He also developed Padlet activities and activities on the online student learning portal to check for understanding and he said most demonstrated that they understood the structure of the noun phrases.

Examples of Noun Phrases

	Premodifiers		HEAD NOUN	Post-modifier
Determiners	**Adjectives**	**Nouns**		
Many	fluffy white		clouds	in the blue sky (prepositional phrase)
A	slim teenaged		girl	wearing a pale-yellow blouse and comfortable shorts (-ing clause)
The	empty	neighbourhood	park	which was just beside the playground (relative clause using 'which', 'who', 'that')

- Determiners: Tells us about the reference or quantity of the noun
- Adjectives: Adds the descriptive details
- Nouns: Categorises the noun further
- Head Noun: What goes in front of a head noun / Most important noun and tells us what the NP is about
- Post-modifier: Occurs after the head noun and gives more information about it

Figure 3.1 Structure of a noun phrase.

Gajen's choice of an authentic text was an interesting one. He opted for an excerpt from the short story 'A Weakness for Chocolate' – part of a collection of Chinese short stories – by David T.K. Wong. The story revolves around the protagonist, Wen-Yee, who finds herself accused of espionage in China during the Cultural Revolution. Enduring relentless interrogations, she maintains her innocence despite harsh conditions, dwindling health and emotional torment. Confined to a bleak cell, she grapples with loneliness, isolation and despair as she longs for freedom and justice. The conditions became worse when she was transferred to a labour camp in a remote part of the country. Wen-Yee faced gruelling work daily, deplorable living conditions and the loss of her physical vitality. Despite the cruelty of her circumstances, she clung to the hope that one day she might uncover the truth behind her unjust imprisonment.

Each authentic text chosen by the different teachers working on our action research project was a purposeful and deliberate choice. In Gajen's case, the ultimate objective was to use noun phrases to better describe a character, and this excerpt lent itself to meet this objective.

Gajen's noun phrase analysis activity required his students to complete the noun phrase analysis table (see Table 3.7) based on the excerpt he had chosen. His choice of the excerpt from 'A Weakness for Chocolate' (see Excerpt 3.5) was an apt one as it contained varied examples of noun phrases (a longer extract from which the following excerpt is from is attached at the end of the chapter):

EXCERPT 3.5

> Wen-Yee woke with a start. She had been dreaming again about her interrogations. Her fingers felt stiff, and her feet were cold. The journey across the Pacific seemed interminable. The thin airline blanket had slipped to

the floor. She retrieved it and wrapped it around herself again. Her head was aching. Her ears, her gums and her bones ached as well. She struggled against the constraint of the seat belt as the cabin lights dimmed. She had never been on a plane before and was glad the seat next to hers was empty, freeing her from the need to respond to conversation and the fear of disturbing anyone by her fidgeting.

Table 3.7 Gajen's noun phrase analysis table for 'A Weakness for Chocolate'.

Premodifiers			Head noun	Postmodifier
Determiners	Adjectives	Nouns		
			start	
			interrogations	
			fingers	
			feet	
			journey	
			blanket	
			floor	
			head	
			ears	
			gums	
			bones	
			constraint	
			lights	
			plane	
			seat	
			need	
			fear	

In an interview excerpt, Gajen emphasised the importance of incorporating authentic Asian texts into his lesson materials. He mentioned that such texts, with their cultural context and inclusion of Asian names and places effectively engaged students, making the content more relatable. Gajen emphasised how these texts, reflecting real-world writing, sparked deeper discussions and reinforced classroom lessons, such as expanding noun phrases, through more tangible, relatable examples.

Reflecting on the post-teaching phase, Gajen felt that the lessons generally went well but thought that if given more time, it would have been more effective. However, he found that his learners did value the lessons and became more aware of noun phrases within sentences in their reading and writing. Thinking more deeply on his participation in the research project, he acknowledged that it had significantly expanded his own grammar knowledge and enhanced his pedagogical content knowledge as a teacher, particularly in teaching grammar in the context of reading and writing.

Gajen shared in his interview that he now has a clearer understanding of how noun phrases function in a text. He disclosed that when marking his students' written pieces, he can better assess their use of noun phrases:

> I think, from a teacher's perspective, when students are writing, you can look at their work and see the use of noun phrases. You might notice that there is deliberate use of postmodifiers rather than just premodifiers. Preparing this lesson package has allowed me to think at that level, which I wouldn't have been able to do previously. So, it was very beneficial.
>
> (Gajen, Interview)

This experience, he shared, has boosted his confidence as a language teacher. He appreciated the stronger focus on emphasising grammar as a tool for meaning making rather than as isolated rules.

Extracts Used in Chapter 3

The following is the extract from the chapter 'Dinner with Father', in *The Evergreen Tea House*, written by David T.K. Wong.

> *Chu Wing-seng occupied a seat between his parents, as if he were some kind of link between them. His mother was dressed in a white linen suit. His father was in shirtsleeves. It occurred to him suddenly that the last time the three of them dined together his mother had also been dressed in white. Why? White was the colour of purity or of mourning. Was a message being conveyed? About what? There was always something strange between his parents, as if a mysterious undercurrent flowed constantly between them. He never managed to figure out whether that was caused by love or by a certain discomfort with each other's company.*
>
> *As he waited patiently for the food to be served, his mind went over the questions about financial and business matters he wanted to put to his father. It would be a pleasant change from the boring topics woven around his studies, his scouting, his next set of examinations and his larger ambitions that formed the staple of conversations with his mother. There would also be respite from those worn out tales about the Lord Buddha's enlightenment under the Bodhi tree, about a Chinese monk's journey to India to acquire holy scriptures, or about Zen masters using impossible parables to defeat the mind. He would have to avoid posing direct questions about*

making money to his father, however, because he knew his mother's temperament and did not want to upset her.

In front of him, the table was laid out with all the formal accessories. Personalised ivory chopsticks with names engraved in red. Polished silver chopstick rests. Little square dishes of sauces and condiments. Embroidered linen napkins, immaculately starched and ironed. A centrepiece filled with fresh pink flowers whose name he did not know. It was a far cry from the simple dinners eaten with his mother in the small alcove in her private quarters.

His mother's vegetarian dishes of tofu, mushrooms, beansprouts and stir-fried pak choi were the first to arrive. Then came the dishes of pork cooked with dried mustard greens, eggs scrambled with shrimps and Chinese broccoli fried with beef seasoned with oyster sauce meant for himself and his father. It occurred to Chu Wing-seng suddenly how ridiculous it was to have two Filipino maids serving three people seated at a table meant for twelve!

The meal proceeded in relative silence, except for Chu Wing-seng's occasional protest when his mother placed a helping of her vegetarian fare into his bowl. After a while, the questioning began.

The following is the extract from the story 'A Weakness for Chocolate' (pp. 2–4), in *Chinese Stories in Times of Change*, written by David T. K. Wong.

Wen-Yee woke with a start. She had been dreaming again about her interrogations. Her fingers felt stiff, and her feet were cold. The journey across the Pacific seemed interminable. The thin airline blanket had slipped to the floor. She retrieved it and wrapped it around herself again. Her head was aching. Her ears, her gums and her bones ached as well. She struggled against the constraint of the seat belt as the cabin lights dimmed. She had never been on a plane before and was glad the seat next to hers was empty, freeing her from the need to respond to conversation and the fear of disturbing anyone by her fidgeting. She clutched a large, worn plastic handbag close to her hollow chest, as if its pressure provided relief from her aches and pains. The bag was filled with all manner of odds and ends, including that tiny, foil wrapped square of milk chocolate retained from her dinner tray.

Two other items in the bag were of particular importance to her – a Green Card from the American immigration authorities, secured by her elder brother, Kee, and the Third Volume of the collected works of Chairman Mao. The former was freshly issued while the latter remained in almost mint condition, in spite of having been in her possession for some twenty-seven years.

Wen-yee's face was creased and leathery from long exposure to the elements. Her long neck, with loose folds of skin like those of a tortoise, was just as leathery. Her left eye was half-blinded with trachoma. She had several teeth missing and her hair had turned prematurely to a dirty white. The hands clasping the antique handbag were twisted with arthritis.

She had been a great beauty once, with a neck as graceful as a swan's. She had been vivacious and outgoing. Her lambent eyes, her playful mouth and her long, silken hair had endowed her with the kind of loveliness that reduced suitors to despair. But that had been long ago, during her age of innocence, and at the time of her friendship with Monica Lamb. Their mutual weakness for Cadbury's chocolates was what had landed her in prison.

She wondered momentarily where Monica might be. No doubt nicely settled somewhere in Somerset, married to that childhood sweetheart she had spoken about. Possibly surrounded by a brood of children. Perhaps she might even be blessed with grandchildren by now.

References

Wong, D.T.K. (2003). Dinner with Father. In *The Evergreen Tea House*. Muse Publishing.

Wong, D.T.K. (2009). A weakness for chocolate. In *Chinese Stories in Times of Change*. Muse Publishing.

4 Verbs and Verb Phrases

Types of Verb Meanings

There are many ways to categorise verbs as we will learn in this chapter. One of the ways verbs may be broadly categorised is according to their meaning. This book adopts the meaning categorisation of verbs as action verbs, linking verbs, saying verbs, sensing verbs and mental verbs, following how Alsagoff (2023) does so. The following illustrates the different verb meanings:

- **Action verbs** – Action verbs are verbs of doing an action. Examples of action verbs are *walk, run, eat, sleep* and *play*. For example, in *Tracey peeled the orange*, the action verb is *peeled* and in *The river flowed to the sea*, the action is *flowed*.
- **Linking verbs** – Linking verbs are verbs of being or relating. A prototypical linking verb is the copular verb *be* (and that is why linking verbs are sometimes referred to as copular verbs) which may be realised in varied forms like *am, is, was* and *were*. Linking verbs behave like '=' signs and typically relate the subject of a clause to a subject complement that describes, defines or identifies the subject. For example, in *The old man is very hardworking*, the linking verb *is* describes *the old man* (the subject realised by a noun phrase) as being *very hardworking* (the subject complement realised by an adjective phrase). There are other linking verbs which behave like '=' signs like the verbs *appear, seems, grew* and *become*. For example, in *The quietest girl in my class became the school council president*, the linking verb *became* identifies *the quietest girl in my class* (the subject realised by a noun phrase) as *the school council president* (the subject complement realised by another noun phrase).
- **Saying verbs** – Saying verbs are verbs of saying or telling. Examples of saying verbs are *say, shout, claim, respond* and *argue*. For example, in *She whispered that she was bored at the party*, the saying verb is *whispered*. Another example is the saying verb *exclaimed* in *Rita exclaimed, 'I won the lucky draw!'*.
- **Sensing verbs** – Sensing verbs, otherwise known as verbs of perception, are verbs related to the five senses – *sight, smell, touch, taste* and *hearing*. For

DOI: 10.4324/9781003255963-4

example, in *Lynette noticed a little yellow bird perched on the tree*, the sensing verb *noticed* is a verb related to the sense of sight. In another example, *I savoured the delicious chocolate cake*, the sensing verb *savoured* is a verb related to the sense of taste.
- **Mental verbs** – Mental verbs are verbs of thinking, knowing and feeling. For example, in The *jury pondered over the verdict*, the verb *pondered* is a verb of thinking. In the example *My mother realised she had lost her keys when she reached the front gate*, the verb *realised* is a verb of knowing. An example of a verb of feeling is in the example *Wei Ling loved her new little kitten*, where the verb *love* is a verb of feeling.

You can find a range of verb meanings – action, linking, saying, sensing and mental – represented through the use of different verbs (for example, there is a range of saying verbs) in this excerpt below from the book titled *The Amazing Komodo Dragon*, written by Fitri Kurniawan. The narrative centres around Maida's family visiting Komodo Island in Indonesia. The range of verb meanings expressed through different verbs makes this text vivid. The main verbs are underlined and analysed in brackets (note: some verbs may be analysed in more than one way, depending on one's perspective. For example, the verb *watching* used here may be analysed as either a sensing or action verb depending on one's perspective of the action).

EXCERPT 4.1

> 'Hurray! Uncle Benny is <u>coming</u> (action) to <u>visit</u> (action) us!' Maida <u>said</u> (saying) while <u>waving</u> (action) the postcard she just <u>received</u> (action) from the postman. 'And what <u>is</u> (linking) more exciting is that Uncle will <u>take</u> (action) us all for holiday. Anywhere we <u>like</u> (mental) !' She <u>yelled</u> (saying) again.
>
> 'Let's <u>go</u> (action) abroad! They <u>have</u> (linking) a lot of sales now!' Kak Neni <u>shouted</u> (saying) from her room. 'What if we <u>go</u> (action) to Komodo Island?' Dad <u>suggested</u> (saying). He was apparently <u>watching</u> (sensing) a TV program about Komodo dragons.
>
> 'Oh no! It must <u>be</u> (linking) dirty and smelly there. Besides, there <u>are</u> (linking) a lot of dinosaurs just everywhere! Gee!' Kak Neni <u>shuddered</u> (action). 'The Komodo dragon <u>is</u> (linking) not a dinosaur, although they also have <u>existed</u> (linking) since the prehistoric time,' Maida <u>explained</u> (saying) <u>imitating</u> (action) Mr. Sofyan, her Biology teacher.
>
> 'Let's <u>vote</u> (action)! The place with most votes <u>wins</u> (action)!' Kak Neni <u>said</u> (saying) confidently. '<u>Shopping</u> (action) somewhere overseas!' Kak Neni <u>said</u> (saying) while <u>raising</u> (action) her hand up in the air.
>
> Dad, Mom, and Kak Berlian <u>looked</u> (sensing) at one another. 'What! Nobody <u>wants</u> (mental) to <u>go</u> (action) abroad?' Kak Neni <u>yelled</u> (saying) disappointedly. '<u>Going</u> (action) to Komodo Island should <u>be</u> (linking) nice,

Nen. Indonesia is (linking) the only country with Komodo dragons. How can we only watch (sensing) them on TV!' Kak Berlian said (saying). 'OK! Komodo Island, here we come (action)!' Kak Neni said (saying) sulkily.

Stative and Dynamic Verbs

Stative Verbs

Another important distinction in the meaning of verbs, in relation to the nature of action or state described, is that between stative and dynamic verbs. Stative verbs describe states. Examples of stative verbs usually include linking, mental and sensing verbs like *be, know, prefer* and *see*. These verbs are usually not observable and cannot be measured by a concrete start or end point. As such, they usually do not take the progressive or continuous form, like the following:

* She is understanding the teacher.
We would say *She understands the teacher.*

* Alex is liking to bake.
We would say *Alex likes to bake.*

However, these stative verbs may be used in the progressive or continuous forms in some cases like the following:

- To express a temporary state or condition
  - *I am loving this pool!*
  - *I am staying in a service apartment while my house is being renovated.*
- To express an active meaning
  - *I'm having a sandwich.* (active meaning: eating)
  - *The boy is being annoying!* (active meaning: behaving)

Dynamic Verbs

Dynamic verbs describe actions which are usually observable and measurable. Examples of dynamic verbs usually include action and saying verbs like *kick, eat, bake, say* and *shout*. Dynamic verbs can take the progressive or continuous forms, like the following:

The children are running to the park excitedly.
While she was sleeping, her phone rang, jolting her awake.

As I *was asking* my teacher for clarification on the assignment, the school bell rang.

Moving on from verb meanings, let's revisit and extend the discussion of verb forms and verb functions introduced in Chapter 2.

Verb Forms

Another way of categorising verbs is through their forms. Most verbs have six different verb forms – the base, the third person singular present tense, the past tense, the progressive or the continuous *-ing* participle, the perfect *-ed/-en* participle and the passive *-ed/-en* participle. It is important to note that not all verbs can take all the forms. For example, a stative verb cannot usually take the progressive or the continuous *-ing* form and an intransitive verb cannot take the passive *-ed/en* form (refer to Chapter 6 for an explanation of what intransitive verbs are). In addition, depending on whether verbs are regular or irregular verbs, the forms may vary.

In regular verbs, the past tense forms and the perfect *-ed/-en* particles end with the *-ed* suffix. Table 4.1 presents some examples.

In irregular verbs, the past tense forms and the perfect *-ed/-en* particles vary. Table 4.2 presents some examples.

The copular verb *be* is the only verb in the English language that has eight forms. The eight forms are shown in Table 4.3.

The different verb forms are elaborated below.

Table 4.1 Verb forms of regular verbs.

verb	base	present tense -s	past tense -ed	-ing participle	-ed/en participle
enjoy	enjoy	enjoys	enjoyed	enjoying	enjoyed
listen	listen	listens	listened	listening	listened
jump	jump	jumps	jumped	jumping	jumped

Table 4.2 Verb forms of irregular verbs.

verb	base	present tense -s	past tense -ed	-ing participle	-ed/en participle
hit	hit	hits	hit	hitting	hit
come	come	comes	came	coming	come
bring	bring	brings	brought	bringing	brought
give	give	gives	gave	giving	given

Table 4.3 Verb forms of copula *be*.

verb	base	present tense -s		past tense -ed		-ing participle	-ed/en participle
be	be	am	first person singular	was	first person singular	being	been
		is	third person singular		third person singular		
		are	second (singular and plural) and third person plural	were	second (singular and plural) and third person plural		

Base Form

The base form of the verb is the form with no inflections, that is, with no prefixes or suffixes. It is also known as the infinitive and may be used either as a bare infinitive or as a *to* infinitive, as in the following:

I helped my sister <u>clean</u> her room. (bare infinitive)
I helped my sister <u>to clean</u> her room. (*to* infinitive)

The base form is also used when a command or a request is made in imperatives like the following:

<u>*Keep*</u> *quiet!*
Please <u>finish</u> your breakfast.

Present Tense Form

The present tense is realised in two ways. The singular present tense form is marked by the *-s* suffix (or *-es* or *-ies*, depending on the spelling of the base verb) and the plural present tense form has no *-s* suffix marking, and so looks like the base or infinitive form, as in the following:

Manju <u>swims</u> in the pool every morning. (singular present tense form)
Peter <u>studies</u> till midnight every day.

They <u>swim</u> in the pool every morning. (plural present tense form)
Peter and his sister <u>study</u> till midnight every day.

Past Tense Form

The past tense form is marked using the *-ed* suffix in regular verbs. The past tense form is realised in different ways in irregular verbs. Some examples are the following:

> We <u>climbed</u> the steep hill carefully. (past tense form in regular verbs)
> Noelle and Ariel <u>rested</u> under the shady tree.
>
> Last week, Weiming <u>brought</u> home a little kitten. (past tense forms in irregular verbs)
> The little bird <u>flew</u> right into my balcony last night.
> My mother <u>put</u> some flowers into the vase this morning.

-ing Participle Form

The *-ing* participle is also referred to as the progressive or continuous participle. Please do bear in mind that not all words ending in *-ing* are verbs with the *-ing* participle form. Some adjectives (for example, *interesting, exciting*) and nouns (for example, *building, painting*) also end with *-ing*. Some examples of verbs with the *-ing* participle form are the following:

> They are <u>running</u> to the school gate because they are late for school.
> While <u>walking</u> to the supermarket, my grandfather tripped and fell.
> <u>Feeling</u> sad, she left the room.

-ed/-en Participle Form

There are two different forms of the *-ed/-en* participle (note: in irregular verbs, the form may vary). One marks the perfect aspect and the other marks the passive voice. A way to distinguish the different forms of the *-ed/-en* participle in finite verb phrases would be to check if the preceding auxiliary verb is a *have/has/had* auxiliary or a *be* auxiliary (note: auxiliaries are elaborated on below). The following are some examples:

> James was not hungry as he <u>had eaten</u> a snack. (*-ed/-en* perfect participle)
> The whole cake <u>was eaten</u> by James. (*-ed/-en* passive participle)
>
> Kiara <u>has cut</u> the greens, so she can put the salad together now. (*-ed/-en* perfect participle)
> The greens <u>were cut</u> by Kiara. (*-ed/-en* passive participle)

Verb Functions

We also said that in terms of function, verbs in a verb phrase may be main (lexical) or auxiliary (helping) verbs. A main verb may stand on its own in a verb phrase or a main verb may have modal or primary auxiliaries precede them in a verb phrase. For example, *should have eaten* is a verb phrase comprising the main verb *eaten* and the modal auxiliary *should* and the primary auxiliary *have*. As discussed in Chapter 2, in a verb phrase, the main verb is obligatory to express an action or a state of being and the auxiliaries which provide additional grammatical information like modality, aspect and voice are optional.

Before we move on to discussing what a verb phrase is and its structure, it is important to understand yet another grammatical distinction between verbs which has to do with the finiteness of a verb, that is, whether the verb is finite or non-finite.

Finite vs Non-Finite Verbs

A finite verb is one that carries tense, person and number. A non-finite verb, on the other hand, does not show contrast in tense, person and number.

Table 4.4 shows some examples of how a verb may be realised as finite or non-finite, using the irregular verb *drive*.

Table 4.4 Finite and non-finite verbs.

Finite	Non-finite

• Present tense
Singular present tense form
  - Meifeng <u>drives</u> her daughters to school every morning.
Plural present tense form
  - Many parents <u>drive</u> their children to school in the morning.
• Past tense
  - Yesterday, Munjoo <u>drove</u> the children to school instead.
	• Base form
	Imperative
	  - <u>Drive</u> slowly!
	Bare infinitive
	  - I watched him <u>drive</u> away.
	To-infinitive
	  - I taught him <u>to drive</u>.
	• Progressive -*ing* form
	  - While <u>driving</u>, it started to rain.
	  - While he was <u>driving</u>, it started to rain.
	• Perfect -*ed/en* form
	  - If he had <u>driven</u> away earlier, I would not have seen him.
	• Passive -*ed/-en* form
	  - The car was <u>driven</u> in a reckless manner.

You will note from the examples that the present and past tense forms of the verbs are finite verbs and the base, the -*ing* participle and the -*ed/-en* participle forms are non-finite verbs.

A finite verb in a sentence will show contrast in tense, person and number if there are changes either in the time reference or subject (in terms of person or number) of the sentence. A non-finite verb will not show contrast in tense, person and number if there are changes in the time reference or the subject (in terms of person or number) of the sentence.

The following verbs are finite because they can change their form to show contrast in tense, number and person.

Contrast in tense (to respond to change in time reference)

- Kaide **walks** to the park *every morning*. (present)
- Kaide **walked** to the park every morning *during her last vacation*. (past)

Contrast in number (to respond to change in subject, whether singular or plural)

- *Linda attends **dance** classes.* (singular)
- *Linda and Mike **attend** dance classes.* (plural)

Contrast in person (to respond to change in subject, whether 1st, 2nd or 3rd person)

- *I **am** excited about the trip.* (1st person)
- *You **are** excited about the trip.* (2nd person)
- *He **is** excited about the trip.* (3rd person)

As mentioned earlier, non-finite verbs do not show contrast in tense, person and number even if there are changes in the time reference or the subject (in terms of person or number) of the sentence. They cannot change their form. The structure of the sentence within which these verbs appear fix the form of these verbs. Before we look at some of these structures that fix the form of these non-finite verbs, it is important to take note that a standalone sentence minimally needs a subject and a finite verb or verb phrase.

The exception to this is the imperative sentence. The imperative sentence gives orders or commands. The base form of the verb is used to form an imperative sentence, usually appearing at the start of the sentence. The doer or the agent, that is, the subject, is also not mentioned (presumed to be *you*). As identified in Table 4.4, the base form of the verb is a non-finite verb, as in the following:

- *Come inside.*
- *Swim ten laps now!*

Besides the imperative sentence structure, there are other sentence structures that fix the form of the non-finite verbs. When main verbs appear in a string one after another in a sentence, forming a chain-like structure, this is known as the catenative construction. The first verb in such a string is a finite verb and the rest of the verbs are non-finite verbs. The first main verb is the catenative verb and these are usually verbs of desire (like *want, wish, love*), verbs of perception (like *see, watch, hear*) and verbs of causation (like *make, help, allow*). Here are some examples:

- *The children want to play in the water.*

The first verb in this catenative construction is the finite verb *want*, which is followed by the non-finite *to*-infinitive verb to *to play*. If we change the plural subject *the children* to a singular subject *the child*, the finite verb changes to show contrast in number, but the non-finite verb remains unchanged as in the following:

- *The child wants to play in the water.*

Here is another example with a catenative construction with an object splitting the string of main verbs:

- *The neighbour <u>saw</u> them <u>climbing</u> the trees.*

The first verb is the finite verb *saw* and this is followed by the non-finite *-ing* participle *climbing*. If we change the time reference of this sentence to present time, it is the finite verb that changes to show contrast in tense, while the non-finite verb remains unchanged as in the following:

- *The neighbour <u>sees</u> them <u>climbing</u> the trees.*

It is also possible to use the bare infinitive instead of the *-ing* participle in these examples:

- *The neighbour <u>saw</u> them <u>climb</u> the trees.*
- *The neighbour <u>sees</u> them <u>climb</u> the trees.*

Even if we change the plural object pronoun *them* to a singular object pronoun like *her* in these examples, there are no changes to the non-finite verbs *climbing* and *climb* as in the following:

- *The neighbour <u>saw</u> her <u>climb</u> the trees.*
- *The neighbour <u>sees</u> her <u>climbing</u> the trees.*

These examples with an object splitting the string of main verbs also show that the verb that follows immediately after an object is a non-finite verb.

Now that we understand the distinction between finite and non-finite verbs, let's look at the structure of a verb phrase.

A Verb Phrase

Like a noun phrase, the structure of a verb phrase may be represented within a table.

In a verb phrase, only the main verb which expresses the actual action or state is obligatory. As mentioned earlier, the modal and primary auxiliaries are optional to add grammatical information like **tense, modality, aspect** and **voice** to the main verb; tense is carried by the first verb in the verb phrase (note: if there is only a main verb in a verb phrase, tense is carried by this main verb); modals like *should, can* and *must* signal meanings of modality; the perfect *have* and the progressive (or continuous) *be* signal meanings of aspect; and the passive *be* signals the passive voice (note: modality, aspect and voice will be elaborated below). While the modal and primary auxiliaries are optional and may be used in any combination (as seen in Table 4.5), they must follow a specific order (note: recall that we said that English is strict about word order in a phrase, very much like how the noun phrase is structured).

Table 4.5 Verb phrase structure.

Modal auxiliary	Primary auxiliary			Main (lexical) verb	Verb phrase
e.g., can, could, may, must, will, would, shall, should, ought to, need to, have to ... (The verb that directly follows must be in its base form)	**HAVE** perfect e.g., has, have, had (The verb that directly follows takes on the -ed/en participle. Therefore, the verb phrase will take, for example, the structure *has + -ed/en*)	**BE** progressive e.g., is, are, was, were, am, been (The verb that directly follows takes on the -*ing* participle. Therefore, the verb phrase will take, for example, the structure *was + -ing*)	**BE** passive e.g., is, are, was, were, am, been (The verb that directly follows takes on the -*ed/en* participle. Therefore, the verb phrase will take, for example, the structure *is + -ed/en*)		
				baked	baked
	has			baked	has baked
		is		baking	is baking
should	have			baked	should have baked
must	have	been		baking	must have been baking
could	have	been	being	baked	could have been being baked (It is not common to have all four auxiliaries used in a verb phrase structure in Standard English)

Let's now consider whether a verb phrase is a finite verb phrase or a non-finite verb phrase. This will be dependent on the first verb in a verb phrase. It is important to note that the auxiliaries are finite verbs. As such, any verb phrase that starts with an auxiliary verb is a finite verb phrase (and by default, all other verbs that follow the first auxiliary in the verb phrase are non-finite verbs). If there is only the obligatory main verb in a verb phrase, and this verb is a finite verb, this is also then a finite verb phrase. The following verb phrases are finite:

- Moorthy <u>should be attending</u> the concert tomorrow.

The modal auxiliary *should* is finite and is followed by non-finite verbs (the bare infinitive *be* and the *-ing* participle *attending*). Because of the auxiliary, the entire verb phrase *should be attending* is finite.

- We <u>have eaten</u> our dinner.

The perfect *have* auxiliary is finite and is followed by a non-finite verb (the *-ed/en* participle *eaten*). Because of the auxiliary, the entire verb phrase *have eaten* is finite.

- Moli <u>played</u> the organ beautifully.

The standalone obligatory main verb *played* is finite in this sentence, and as such, the verb phrase *played* is finite.

If a verb phrase starts with a non-finite verb, that verb phrase is non-finite. If there is only the obligatory main verb in a verb phrase, and this verb is a non-finite verb, this is also then a non-finite verb phrase. Let's identify and discuss non-finite verb phrases in the following examples:

- While <u>running</u>, Irfan <u>tripped</u> on a stone and he <u>fell</u>.

There are, in fact, three verb phrases in this sentence. The three verb phrases are *running*, *tripped* and *fell*. The *-ing* participle *running* is a non-finite verb, and so *running* is a non-finite verb phrase. The other two verb phrases *tripped* and *fell* are finite verb phrases.

- <u>Woken</u> by the sound of her alarm, Ivonne <u>climbed</u> out of bed reluctantly.

There are two verb phrases in this sentence. They are *woken* and *climbed*. The passive *-ed/en woken* is a non-finite verb and so *woken* is a non-finite verb phrase. The other verb phrase *climbed* is a finite verb phrase.

- Anna <u>persuaded</u> her father <u>to give</u> her to more money.

Again, there are two verb phrases in this sentence. The two verb phrases are *persuaded* and *to give*. The verb *persuaded* is a finite verb and so is a finite verb phase. The *to*-infinitive *to give* is a non-finite verb and so is a non-finite verb phrase.

At this point, it is important to note that while modals cannot function as main verbs, primary auxiliaries may also function as main verbs. Let's see how the verbs *have*, *be* and *do* can function as primary auxiliaries and as main verbs in Table 4.6:

Table 4.6 Verbs *have*, *be* and *do* as primary auxiliaries and main verbs.

have, *be* and *do* as primary auxiliaries	*have*, *be* and *do* as main verbs
Aishah <u>has sprained</u> her ankle and so cannot go hiking. (the main verb is *sprained* and the verb *has* is the perfect auxiliary)	Melody <u>has</u> a beautiful garden. (the main verb *has* indicates the meaning of possession)
Denise <u>is running</u> in the marathon. (the main verb is *running* and the verb *is* is the progressive auxiliary)	Christopher <u>is</u> the best chef in town. (the main verb *is* behaves as a linking verb that links the subject, Christopher, to an identity)
The surprise birthday party <u>was planned</u> by my daughters. (the main verb is *planned* and the verb *was* marks the passive voice)	Wei Ming <u>was</u> very excited about the new movie. (the main verb *was* behaves as a linking verb that links the subject, Wei Ming, to an attribute)
Nitya <u>did</u> not <u>like</u> the lemon tarts. (the main verb is *like* and the verb *did* is an auxiliary verb that supports the negative 'not') <u>Do</u> you <u>like</u> those flowers? (the main verb is *like* and the verb *do* is an auxiliary verb that supports the formation of the question) Note: The auxiliary verb *do* is also known as the dummy or empty auxiliary as it has no particular meaning, being used when the sentence construction needs an auxiliary (helping) verb.	Beverly <u>did</u> her daily exercise this morning. (the main verb *did* is an action verb that means to complete)

Before elaborating on the role of modal and primary auxiliary verbs in terms of modality, aspect and time, let's discuss tense and time.

Tense and Time

In the English language, there are only two tenses – the present and the past tenses. The **tense** of a verb is a grammatical marking on a verb. In the English language, only the present and the past tenses are marked in verbs – the present tense is typically marked by the *-s* suffix and the past tense is typically marked by the *-ed* suffix. Tense in a verb phrase is carried by the first verb in the verb phrase. If the verb phrase comprises only the main verb, the tense of the verb phrase is marked by the main verb, that is, by 'the *-s* to signal the present tense or the *-ed* to signal the past tense. This marking is, of course, dependent on whether the main verb is a regular (for example, *walked* and *pulled*) or an irregular verb (for example, *flew* and *went*) or whether the verb is plural or singular (for example, *Minah sleeps* vs *Minah and Mira sleep*). If the verb phrase comprises one or more auxiliary verbs, the tense of the verb phrase is signalled by the first auxiliary verb, for example, the present tense is signalled by *is* in the verb phrase *is eating* and the past tense is signalled by *had* in the verb phrase *had been eating*.

In the English language, there is no future tense as there is no grammatical marking in the English language on the verb to signal the future tense. However, clearly, we can talk about events or states of being in the future time. To express events or states of being in the future time, we use other ways, including using the present and the past tense. As such, there is a distinction between tense (present and past) and time (present, past and future).

Below, we present some of the meanings expressed using the present tense, with some examples.

The following uses of the present tense refer to present time:

- Factual present
    - The present tense is used to express statements as facts and timeless truths (sometimes referred to as 'timeless present').
        - *The capital of Vietnam is Hanoi.* (fact)
        - *The sun rises in the east and sets in the west.* (timeless truth)
        - *Water boils at 100°C.* (timeless truth)

- Habitual present
    - The present tense is used to express repeated events. An adverbial of time expressing frequency is usually used alongside as well.
        - *I go for a morning walk at the Singapore Botanic Gardens every Saturday morning.*
        - *We have lunch with our grandparents every Sunday.*
        - *Every year, the Chia family visits Japan during the June school holidays.*

- Instantaneous present
  - The present tense is used to express events happening at the moment of speech, like news broadcasts or demonstrations.
    - *Police <u>line</u> the streets as the demonstrators march forward.* (live news broadcast)
    - *I <u>mix</u> the glitter with the glue.* (arts and craft demonstration)

The following uses of the present tense refer to past or future time:

- Historic present
  - The present tense is used to refer to past events. When the present tense is used this way, events, though passed, are presented as if they were in the present, conveying immediacy or drama to the events.
    - *Powerful aftershocks <u>jolt</u> the island.* (newspaper headline)
    - *Ronaldo <u>kicks</u> the ball towards the goal!* (sports commentary)
    - *The young soldier <u>draws</u> his gun at the first sound of gunfire.* (narrative)
- Planned future event
  - The present tense is used to refer to events, typically pre-planned, taking place in the future time. An adverbial of time indicating future time is usually used as well.
    - *The school children <u>leave</u> for the school trip next Tuesday.*
    - *Taylor Swift <u>is arriving</u> in Singapore tomorrow!*

Below, we present some of the meanings expressed using the past tense, with some examples.

The following uses of the past tense refer to past time:

- Past event
  - The past tense is used to refer to past events that happened at a specific time. The past tense is also used to refer to past events that happened repeatedly. An adverbial of time indicating the specific time is usually used as well.
    - *The entire village <u>celebrated</u> the wedding of the young couple last March.*
    - *Thanh Ha <u>visited</u> her grandparents in Vietnam yearly.* (repeated past action)

The following uses of the past tense refer to present time:

- Attitudinal past
  - The past tense is used to express the speaker's or writer's present attitude or emotional state.
    - *I <u>knew</u> we would win the debate!*
    - *I <u>was</u> excited to try the new restaurant that just opened.*

- Politeness past
    - The past tense is used to sound more polite in the present time.
        - I *was hoping* we could go to the concert together. (less direct than *Let's go to the concert together*)
        - I *wanted* a cup of coffee. (less demanding than *I want a cup of coffee*)

The following uses of the past tense refer to a hypothetical future time:

- Hypothetical future
    - The past tense is used to express a hypothetical or imaginary situation that could happen in the future. The conditional *if*-clauses are usually used here.
        - If I *won* the lottery, I would buy myself a car.
        - If it *snowed* tomorrow, the children would be thrilled.

The following uses of the past tense in indirect or reported speech to refer to events in present time in direct speech:

- Sylvia said 'I *am* so tired' – Sylvia said that she *was* so tired.
- The choir conductor said, 'We *are practising* hard for the Christmas concert' – The choir conductor said that they *were practising* hard for the Christmas concert.

The following are some of the other ways events taking place in future time may be expressed (apart from the use of the present and past tense), usually accompanied by adverbials of time indicating future time:

- Use of modals (especially the modal *will*)
    - I *will* let you know my decision on Tuesday.
    - Rachel *will* be submitting her assignment in the afternoon.
    - I *shall* call you tomorrow.
    - The parcel *should* arrive by Friday.
    - Hidayah *may* attend the performance.

- Use of *be going to*
    - Ethan *is going to start* his new job next month.
    - The school *is going to announce* the class champion tomorrow.

- Use of *be to* or *be about to*
    - My cousin *is to visit* us this coming June.
    - We *are about to go* for a swim. Do you want to join us?

In the sections below, we elaborate on how the modal and primary auxiliary verbs add a range of meanings to the main verb.

Modality

Modal auxiliaries or modals express a range of modality meanings such as permission, obligation, possibility and ability. Using modals, writers and speakers can qualify their statements or hedge their statements or claims in varying degrees, instead of presenting these as absolute truths. The main meanings of modals are as follows (note: included in the examples are semi-modals like *ought to*, *have to* and *be able to*):

- Permission
    - *You may leave the room.*
    - *The children can go to the playground.*
    - *Could we attend the concert, please?*

- Obligation
    - *I should help my mother with the household chores.*
    - *He ought to apologise to her for his mean words.*
    - *The class must finish the assignment by the end of the week.*
    - *I have to finish the vegetables on my plate.*

- Possibility
    - *Anyone can win the grand prize in the lucky draw.*
    - *Elena could change her mind and attend the party after all.*
    - *My brother may be wrong about the directions to the restaurant.*

- Probability
    - *It might rain heavily.*
    - *It may rain heavily.*
    - *It will rain heavily.*

(Note: these express degrees of certainty of an event likely happening. Using *will* is more certain than *may* and using *may* is more certain than *might*.)

- Ability
    - *Sharon can swim now.*
    - *Sharon could not swim five years ago.*
    - *I am able to attend the committee meeting next week.*

We mentioned earlier that the first verb in a verb group will signal the tense of the verb phrase. If there is a modal auxiliary in a verb phrase, it will take the first position in a verb phrase. So does a modal auxiliary signal tense? Traditional grammar sometimes distinguishes pairs of modals as signalling the present vs. the past, for example, *can* vs. *could*, *may* vs. *might* and *shall* vs. *should*. From the examples shared, it is clear that modals express a range of nuances of meanings, not tied to the signalling of the present and the past tense. From the examples, the only pair of examples that signals the present vs. the past is when the modal *can* in *Sharon can swim now* signals present ability and *could* in *Sharon could not swim five years ago* signals past ability. The only time when the distinction between present and past tense in the use of modal auxiliaries is clear is in the use of direct and indirect speech. For example,

Mary said, 'He may attend badminton practice tomorrow.'

Mary said he might attend badminton practice the next day.

Aspect

Aspect refers to perspective, that is, *how* a writer or speaker experiences, views and conveys an action taking place in relation to time, specifically in terms of whether the action is complete, ongoing or showing duration. This contrasts with tense which has more to do with the distinction between the present and the past. To indicate aspect, we use the perfect *have* and the progressive (or continuous) *be*.

Let's first discuss the perfect aspect. The perfect aspect is used to describe actions which happened at some time in the past and relate them to a reference point in the present time (present perfect) or to a reference point in the past time (past perfect).

(Note: the discussion below introduces the terms 'simple present' and 'simple past'. The simple present and the simple past are verb forms that do not express the perfect or the progressive aspects.)

Present Perfect

The simple past and the present perfect is usually contrasted. The simple past is used to convey an action that took place at a specific point in past time. The present perfect is used to convey that something happened in the past and still has some current relevance to the present time. The 'current relevance' could be that the action or fact still holds true, the action has direct implications to the present or the action was recently completed. Different time adverbials are used in conveying the simple past and the present perfect.

- *Shilpa lived* [simple past] *in Sydney till 2020.* (She does not live there anymore.)
- *They have lived* [present perfect] *in Sydney since 2016.* (They still live there.)

- *Harvinder sprained* [simple past] *her foot last week.* (The action happened last week and has no relevance to the present.)
- *Raphael has sprained* [present perfect] *his foot and so will not be able to take part in the games.* (The action happened some time in the past and has relevance to the present.)

- *The principal _announced_* [simple past] *the winner of the competition last week.* (The action was completed last month.)
- *The government _has announced_* [present perfect] *plans for financial assistance packages.* (The action was just recently completed – this is common in news reporting.)

Past Perfect

The past perfect is used to relate an earlier (or more distant) past action or state to a later-occurring past action or state. The past perfect is sometimes referred to as 'the earlier past' or 'the past of the past'.

- *Samuel _had finished_ his homework by the time he went to the playground.* (the earlier past action is *had finished*)
- *I _had left_ the birthday party before the magician arrived.* (the earlier past action is *had left*)

The excerpt that Gajen used to teach his students noun phrases as discussed in Chapter 3 (from 'A Weakness for Chocolate' written by David T.K. Wong) has examples of the use of the past perfect.

EXCERPT 4.2

> Wen-Yee woke with a start. She _had been dreaming_ again about her interrogations. Her fingers felt stiff and her feet were cold. The journey across the Pacific seemed interminable. The thin airline blanket _had slipped_ to the floor. She retrieved it and wrapped it around herself again. Her head was acing. Her ears, her gums and her bones ached as well. She struggled against the constraint of the seat belt as the cabin lights dimmed. She _had_ never _been_ on a plane before and was glad the seat next to hers was empty, freeing her from the need to respond to conversation and the fear of disturbing anyone by her fidgeting.

The past perfects used in the excerpt (underlined) convey earlier past actions in relation to the narration told. The past perfect progressive *had been dreaming* conveys that Wen-Yee was dreaming before she woke with a start. The past perfect *had slipped* also indicates that the blanket slipped off Wen-Yee before she woke with a start. The past perfect *had . . . been* used in *She had never been on a plane before* adds a biographical (or retrospective) background to understand Wen-Yee's even further past experiences. In the use of the first two past perfects in this excerpt, you will note that there is no need to use time adverbials like 'before' or 'earlier' to sequence the events. The use of the simple past and the past perfect may be used to convey the sequence of events in a text, without the explicit use of time adverbials.

Let's now discuss the progressive aspect. The progressive aspect generally describes ongoing (and not completed) actions at a given time.

Present Progressive

When the present progressive is used, the ongoing action is described in the present time to describe the duration of an action, the temporary nature of an action, or an action that is taking place at the time of speaking:

- The Wongs *are travelling* around Europe for two months. (duration of an action)
- We *are living* with friends while waiting for the keys to our new home. (temporary nature of an action)
- I *am perspiring* in the heat! (action taking place at the time of speaking)

The present progressive may also be used to describe a planned action in the future time:

- The Kannans *are visiting* us next month.

Past Progressive

When the past progressive is used, the ongoing action is described in the past time to describe the temporary nature of an action, the repeated nature of an action, the simultaneous actions happening, the interruption of an action by another action or the background for another action:

- I *was using* a rental car while waiting for my car to be repaired. (temporary nature of an action)
- She *was running* for an hour every morning for six months. (repeated nature of an action)
- While I *was singing*, Edith was playing the piano. (simultaneous actions happening)
- My mother *was mopping* the floor when the doorbell rang. (interruption of an action by another action)
- Anne *was studying* late into the night when the lights suddenly went out. (background for another action)

The present progressive and the past progressive may be contrasted with the use of the simple present and the simple past respectively to convey differences in how actions are perceived:

- James *sings* beautifully. (simple present to convey that he is a good singer generally)
- James *is singing* beautifully. (present progressive to convey that he is a good singer during that time)

- I *wrote* a letter to my cousin in Thailand yesterday. (simple past to convey that the letter is completed)
- I *was writing* a letter to my cousin in Thailand yesterday. (past progressive to convey that the letter may not yet be completed)

The perfect and the progressive may be used together to convey some of the following meanings:

The present perfect progressive may be used to describe an action that started in the past but still continues to the present and may be ongoing:

- Yuni <u>has been playing</u> the piano since she was five years old.
- I <u>have been waiting</u> for the bus for 20 minutes now.

The past perfect progressive may be used to describe an action that was ongoing in an earlier past time up to another action in a later past time:

- We <u>had been living</u> in Singapore before my father got a job in Japan.
- The roads were flooded in the morning because it <u>had been raining</u> heavily the whole night.

The following set of examples illustrates the difference between tense and aspect:

- When I reached home, the rain <u>stopped</u>.
- When I reached home, the rain <u>was stopping</u>.
- When I reached home, the rain <u>had stopped</u>.

All the underlined verb phrases in the above examples are in the past tense, which means the actions happened before the present time. However, the aspect of the underlined verb phrases differs, changing the perspective of the action of the rain in relation to the action of reaching home. In the first instance, the use of the simple past *stopped* conveys that the rain stopped at the point the writer reached home. In the second instance, the use of the past progressive *was stopping* conveys that it was still raining (though reducing in precipitation) when the writer reached home. In the third instance, the use of the past perfect *had stopped* conveys that the rain stopped before the writer reached home. The different aspectual choices then convey different perspectives on how the actions played out in the past.

Voice

Verbs (more specifically, verbs that require objects – transitivity of verbs is discussed in Chapter 6) can be in the active or passive voice. A verb phrase in the passive voice must contain the passive *-ed/-en* participle (as you will note in the examples below).

When a verb is expressed in the **active voice** in a clause, the focus is on the doer or the agent of the action:

- the doer or the agent of the action is the subject of the clause and
- the undergoer or the patient of the action is the object of the clause.

Let's look at a clause in the active voice:

The cat ate the rat.

In this clause, *the cat* is the agent of the action and so is the subject of the clause, and *the rat* is the undergoer or the patient of the action and so is the object of the clause.

If we wish to focus on the patient of the action or wish to not mention the agent of the action, we can express the verb in the **passive voice** in the clause. In this case,

- the patient of the action becomes the subject of the clause and
- the agent of the action is either in a *by*-phrase or omitted.

The clause in the passive voice is as follows:

The rat was eaten (by the cat).

The *by*-phase is in brackets because this is optional. We can also just say *The rat was eaten*. When we choose to omit the by-phrase in a passive clause, we avoid mentioning the agent of the action. We might choose not to mention the agent (the doer) for various reasons like the following:

- The agent is unknown or the identity of the agent is uncertain. When newspapers report crimes, and the offenders are unknown, the passive voice is usually used.
  - *The shop on Iskandar Street had been robbed.*
  - *The victim's personal information was accessed during the data breach.*
- The writer or speaker does not wish to ascribe blame to the agent. To avoid sounding accusatory, the writer or speaker can use the passive voice.
  - *The vase was broken when I came home.*
  - *The project was mismanaged, resulting in a loss of income for the company.*
- The agent is not the focus. In explanation texts, for example, the focus is usually on the process, and not the agent or the doer. In explaining the process of chocolate-making for example, you might find the following as part of the process:
  - *The cocoa beans are harvested and then are dried. Next, the cocoa beans are roasted. After that, the shells of the cocoa beans are removed. The cocoa nibs which are found inside are then ground into fine paste.*
- The agent is common or universal knowledge.
  - *The internet is being used for many reasons like communication, research and business.*
  - *Volcanoes are formed at the boundaries of tectonic plates.*

Verb Phrases as Meaning Making in Texts

Types of Verbs as Meaning Making

The introductory chapter of *Where's Grandma?* is rich with action verbs of movement that serve to contrast the two main characters –elderly Grandma and young Luke. Some of these verbs of movement (or action verbs generally) that contrast the two characters are underlined:

EXCERPT 4.3

'Alright, give me a minute,' she said as she <u>shuffled</u> to get her walking stick.
  Thin and tall, Grandma <u>walked</u> slowly but steadily to the door. I held her arm as we <u>walked</u> towards the lift and kept the door open as Grandma <u>tottered</u> inside.
  For the past month, we had not been to the playground. Instead, we went to the neighbourhood park. For fifteen minutes every day, we would <u>stroll</u> together so that Grandma could get some fresh air and light exercise.

EXCERPT 4.4

When I was little, Grandma took me to the nearby playground every evening. She would hold my hand as we <u>walked</u> through the void decks and car parks.
  When we <u>approached</u> the playground, I would <u>dash</u> to the swings and then feel Grandma's warm palms pushing my back as I <u>soared</u> into the sky.

EXCERPT 4.5

Things changed after the fall. It was Grandma who <u>fell</u>. While coming out of the toilet, Grandma <u>slipped</u> and <u>crashed</u> onto the floor. Kaboonk!
  I <u>dashed</u> to the toilet. Grandma was groaning softly. Blood oozed from a deep gash on her forehead. She had also sprained her left ankle. That happened almost two months ago. Although Grandma recovered, she <u>walks</u> with a slight limp and a walking stick.

Action verbs that indicate quick movements (for example, *dashed* and *soared*) are used to describe Luke, while action verbs that indicate slow movements (for example, *shuffled* and *tottered*) are used to describe Grandma. Even when the neutral action verb 'walk' is used in relation to Grandma, it is modified through the use adverbials like *slowly but steadily* and *with a slight limp and a walking stick*. This contrasts both the characters, painting Luke as energetic and Grandma as struggling with her mobility because of her old age, or a past injury. The verbs used to describe Grandma evoke empathy in the reader.
  The only instances when action verbs indicating quick movements are used in relation to Grandma is when she fell. The action verbs like *fell*, *slipped*

Verbs and Verb Phrases 73

and *crashed* describe the impact of Grandma's fall, setting the scene then for Grandma's deterioration in health and struggle with Alzheimer's disease.

Tense and Aspect as Meaning Making

EXCERPT 4.6

> *Things <u>changed</u> after the fall. It <u>was</u> Grandma who <u>fell</u>. While <u>coming</u> out of the toilet, Grandma <u>slipped</u> and <u>crashed</u> onto the floor. Kaboonk!*
>
> *I <u>dashed</u> to the toilet. Grandma <u>was groaning</u> softly. Blood <u>oozed</u> from a deep gash on her forehead. She <u>had</u> also <u>sprained</u> her left ankle. That <u>happened</u> almost two months ago. Although Grandma <u>recovered</u>, she <u>walks</u> with a slight limp and a walking stick.*

This short excerpt is rich in how tense and aspect are used to move actions or events back and forth in time, conveying different perspectives on the temporal flow of these actions or events.

The use of the simple past conveys completed actions or events that happened at a single point in the past, and when the simple past is used in a consecutive manner, a chronological sequence of events is also usually described (if there are no time adverbials to suggest otherwise). For example, in expressing the following,

> *Grandma <u>slipped</u> and <u>crashed</u> onto the floor. Kaboonk!*
>
> *I <u>dashed</u> to the toilet. Grandma was groaning softly. Blood <u>oozed</u> from a deep gash on her forehead.*

the use of the simple past *slipped*, *crashed*, *dashed* and *oozed* suggests that these completed, single-point events happened in the past in this particular sequential order. There is a narrative progression here, suggesting the cause and effect of particular events here.

There is one use of the simple present here, with the use of the verb *walks*. The use of the simple present reorientates the recount to the present time, within which the writer is recounting the past. The use of the simple past and present in the text allows the reader to move back and forth in situating the events in time.

In terms of the use of aspect, there is the use of the past progressive *was groaning* and the past perfect *had . . . sprained* in the excerpt. Let's discuss why the writer has chosen to use these aspectual contrasts in this text.

The use of the past progressive *was groaning* describes the scene of what Grandma was doing when Luke ran to the toilet to check on her. Grandma was in the process of groaning in pain when Luke reached the toilet. The use of the past progressive conveys an ongoing action and makes the scene more vivid for the readers.

The use of the past perfect *had . . . sprained* sequences the action of spraining as an earlier past event to the action of Luke dashing (signalled using the simple past *dashed*) to the toilet and the action of the blood oozing (signalled using the simple past *oozed*). Notice that there is no explicit use of any time adverbials here to indicate the sequence of events. The sequencing of events is achieved using the past perfect. This helps readers follow the flow and sequence of the events in the excerpt.

There is also the use of the non-finite progressive verb *coming* in the non-finite subordinate clause *While coming out of the toilet* in the sentence, *While coming out of the toilet, Grandma slipped and crashed onto the floor*. Why the choice to use a non-finite subordinate clause? The choice to use the non-finite subordinate clause, with no explicit mention of the subject, Grandma, could be to create some sort of suspense for the readers, making them wonder what is going to happen. Compare the use of the non-finite verb *coming* with the possible use of the finite verb phrase 'was coming':

> *It was Grandma who fell. While [Grandma was] coming out of the toilet, Grandma slipped and crashed onto the floor.*

With the use of the finite verb phrase 'was coming', the element of suspense is removed with the needed introduction of the subject, *Grandma*. In addition, there will be the repetition of *Grandma*. *Grandma* is mentioned in the main clause before (*It was Grandma who fell*) and the main clause that comes after (*Grandma slipped and crashed onto the floor*). Hence, the choice to use the non-finite verb *coming* in the subordinate clause is more effective here.

Exploring 'Saying Verbs' with 10-Year-Olds

Let us explore TAnne's approach to introducing saying verbs to her group of 10-year-old students. TAnne is a seasoned English teacher with extensive teaching experience. Situated in the Western part of the island, her school is a typical primary school located within one of Singapore's suburban public housing estates. TAnne has been teaching at this school for many years, bringing her wealth of knowledge and expertise to her classroom.

With her current class of students, whom she describes as middle-readiness learners, TAnne saw a need to revisit the concept of saying verbs. This decision stemmed from a recent writing task where TAnne observed a gap in her students' usage of these verbs which indicated an area for improvement. Although her students read stories, they rarely identified and applied suitable words or phrases from their reading to their writing. Additionally, they tended to overuse mundane words, particularly saying verbs like 'said' and 'asked'. Another objective was to have her students appreciate Asian texts more.

TAnne opted for the authentic Asian text 'The Island' by writer Lee Su Kim. This tale is part of Lee's anthology *Kebaya Tales*, a compilation of short stories delving into the lives of individuals within the Peranakan community in Malaysia. Set against the backdrop of a boat journey to Pulau Besar, an island off the coast of Mersing, Johor, Malaysia, 'The Island' weaves together local beliefs and superstitions with comedic elements.

TAnne planned a two-hour intervention lesson which took place between drafts one and two of the writing process. The intervention was aimed to effect substantial improvements in their writing. Despite recognising their earnest efforts, TAnne discerned a recurring tendency among the students to heavily rely on commonplace saying verbs such as 'said' and 'asked'. This reliance, she observed, limited the depth of character portrayal and failed to adequately convey the more complex dynamics between characters – as portrayed so effectively in 'The Island'. Eager to facilitate a more nuanced and engaging writing style, TAnne resolved to introduce her students to a more diverse array of saying verbs, and in doing so, encouraging clearer and more impactful storytelling.

The flow of TAnne's two-hour intervention lesson is outlined below.

Reading Comprehension

- Analysing the introduction
  - Understanding the setting, for example, religious practices and use of Malay words
    - *No pork. Anybody here got bring pork?* **Tolong buang.** *Throw away.*
  - Character profiles, for example, choice of words hint at relationship between characters.
    - *thingies perpetually stuck in their ears*
  - Potential Conflict
    - For example, *Throw away. Or else I not going to the island. And you not going too.*

Appreciating Asian Texts

- Comparing 'The Island' with *Frindle* by Andrew Clements (a text which they had done prior to this lesson)

Grammar and Vocabulary

- Choice of words plays an important part in plot development. Getting students to enact two possible scenarios – the boatman using 'said' rather than 'warned'
  - For example, '*Jangan main-main*' he [**said** vs **warned**], '*the spirits on Pulau Besar are powerful*'.

- Grammar – recapitulate the types of verbs
  - The role a verb plays in a sentence
  - How saying verbs affect characterisation and relationships between characters
    - For example, *I said to them* vs *I snapped at them*; *Mum said* vs *Mum scolded*; *Brendan said* vs *Brendan retorted*

Writing – Improving Draft 1

- Show three sample drafts to students. Students are invited to suggest alternative saying verbs and how these improve the writing.
- Apply to their own drafts.

TAnne managed to seamlessly integrate reading, writing, vocabulary and grammar to provide a more holistic learning experience for her students. By introducing the authentic Asian text, 'The Island', TAnne not only exposed her students to diverse cultural perspectives but also fostered a deeper appreciation for literature from the region. Through a targeted reading comprehension activity, TAnne encouraged her students to analyse the introduction for setting, character profiles and potential conflicts. By actively engaging with techniques like the use of non-standard English (*Anybody here got bring pork? Or else I not going to the island*) and Malay words and phrases (*Tolong buang, Jangan main-main*), students gained a deeper understanding of how writers develop the flavour of a narrative. TAnne explained her rationale in the interview: 'I also wanted them to appreciate Asian stories. I wanted them to understand that setting, context, relationships and things like that were important in writing'. In a later part of the interview, she said, 'because it was an Asian text and there were some Malay words in there, my Malay students got quite excited about it. The first thing that stood out was the name of the island, *Jalan Berseh*. So I asked them for the meaning of *berseh*. And the children could tell me.'

Throughout the lessons, TAnne emphasised the significance of grammar and vocabulary in shaping meaning and the impact on writing. She guided her students in understanding how types of verbs and the choice of words could enhance characterisations and shed light on the dynamics between characters. Specifically, TAnne focused on the meaning-making potential of saying verbs, demonstrating how a subtle shift in choice could convey more nuanced emotions and relationships within the text.

Taking her students through a close reading of the text, TAnne effectively showed the impact of these subtle shifts with a series of examples where she replaced the original saying verb in the text with the more neutral *said* (see Excerpt 4.7, 4.8 and 4.9). She then followed with a series of questions probing at a deeper understanding of the text and its characters.

Verbs and Verb Phrases 77

EXCERPT 4.7

Tweaked	Original
'Hey, did you two hear what he said?' I <u>said</u> at them and tried to pull the ear plugs out of the twin standing next to me. He ducked and stuck out a reddish, sugar-coated tongue at me. Mum <u>said</u>, 'Cindy, leave them alone. Let them enjoy themselves.'	'Hey, did you two hear what he said?' I <u>snapped</u> at them and tried to pull the ear plugs out of the twin standing next to me. He ducked and stuck out a reddish, sugar-coated tongue at me. Mum <u>scolded</u>, 'Cindy, leave them alone. Let them enjoy themselves.'

Questions:

1. How did the narrator feel when she said 'Hey, did you two hear what he said?'
2. How did the Mum feel? What was her mood like?
3. How would you describe the relationship between the characters?

EXCERPT 4.8

Tweaked	Original
'Who sez so? I've been to the pyramids of Egypt and the ruins of Angkor,' Damien the smart aleck <u>said</u>. 'Yeah, I've shot savages from my jet plane! And bomb terrorists in the deserts!' Brendan <u>said</u>. 'In front of the PC without moving your lazy bums? Yeah, right,' I <u>said</u>.	'Who sez so? I've been to the pyramids of Egypt and the ruins of Angkor,' Damien the smart aleck <u>shot back</u>. 'Yeah, I've shot savages from my jet plane! And bomb terrorists in the deserts!' Brendan <u>retorted</u>. 'In front of the PC without moving your lazy bums? Yeah, right,' I <u>scoffed</u>.

Questions:

1. What else could you say about the characters of Damien and Brendan?
2. How would you describe the relationship between the characters now?

EXCERPT 4.9

Tweaked	Original
'Do you guys even know what nature means?' 'Nature? Nature means hot, sticky and sweaty. Yechh! Hey, Sis, are you sure you want to go to this island? Think of the mozzies! No toilet . . . you will have to dig a hole or do it in the lalang . . . yucckk . . . think of the leeches coming for you, Ha ha ha!' Brendan <u>said to</u> me.	'Do you guys even know what nature means?' 'Nature? Nature means hot, sticky and sweaty. Yechh! Hey, Sis, are you sure you want to go to this island? Think of the mozzies! No toilet . . . you will have to dig a hole or do it in the lalang . . . yucckk . . . think of the leeches coming for you, Ha ha ha!' Brendan <u>teased</u> me.

Damien <u>said</u>, 'An island, Dad? Awww, who needs to go to an island Dad? I can just google it for you. It's like the real thing. Virtual island, no sweat. Save on petrol, Dad.'	Damien <u>whined</u>, 'An island, Dad? Awww, who needs to go to an island Dad? I can just google it for you. It's like the real thing. Virtual island, no sweat. Save on petrol, Dad.'

Questions:

1. What else could you say about the characters of Damien and Brendan?
2. How would you describe the relationship between the twins and the narrator?

TAnne's activity was a highly effective one. By comparing the original excerpts with those that were replaced with *said* and asking probing questions, TAnne was able to raise awareness of how saying verbs affect characterisation and relationships between characters. This technique not only highlights the impact of the verb choice but also encourages students to think critically about the language they use in their writing. By analysing the different saying verbs (in contrast with *said*) used by the narrator, students would be able to see how the choice of different saying verbs can alter the tone and dynamics of a scene, leading to a deeper understanding of narrative techniques and hopefully more nuanced writing.

In the writing component, TAnne guided her students in applying their newfound insights to their own drafts, encouraging them to experiment with alternative saying verbs to enrich their narratives. This hands-on approach not only reinforced learning but also empowered students to become more confident and expressive writers.

By seamlessly integrating various language skills and using an authentic Asian text, TAnne successfully created a lively learning environment where most of her students grasped concepts effectively. Through her guidance, they were better able to apply a more diverse range of saying verbs to their drafts.

Exploring Aspect with 14-Year-Olds

In this next section, we see Said working with his class of 14-year-old learners. Said works in a secondary school which is situated in the Western side of Singapore. He has been teaching English for a number of years. Said's students live mainly in the public housing which surrounds the school. He shares that this group of students are middle-readiness learners.

Rather than teaching the concept of the past perfect as a standalone grammatical form, Said decided to integrate the purposeful teaching of the past perfect into his series of literacy lessons, effectively illustrating its significance in comprehension, communication and ultimately linking grammar to the writing of narratives.

The following is Said's activity flow across two lessons.

Introducing the Text

- Introducing the text 'Red, Amber, Green'
- Time for individual reading

Discussing and Annotating the Text

- Initiating discussion about students' interpretations of the meaning of the text as well as the sequence of events
- Annotating of text and emphasising the sequence of events

Introducing the Past Perfect

- Introducing past perfect for clarity in sequences
- Checking for understanding, narrowing down to the use of 'had'

Padlet Activity – Discovery

- Conducting Padlet activity to reinforce understanding of the past perfect
- Extracting sentences, discussing past perfect usage

Applying to Writing

- Applying past perfect in narrative writing
- Emphasising purposeful use in essays

Contextualising within Existing Unit of Work

- Relating the lesson to the existing unit of work, focusing on role models
- Students applying past perfect in their narratives

Like the other teachers, Said's approach to teaching grammar as a meaning-making resource was one that attempted to contextualise the teaching of grammar within an authentic Asian text. He focused on aspect – in particular, the use of the past perfect in David T.K. Wong's 'Red, Amber, Green'. The short story explores the themes of cultural identity, assimilation and the immigrant experience. The story follows the protagonist, Old Mak, who as a young boy, journeyed from a small village in Kwangtung Province to Hong Kong for a better life. The story traces his life in Hong Kong and the challenges he faced grappling with the tension between preserving his old ways of life and adapting to the norms of his adopted home. The title, 'Red, Amber, Green,' most likely references a traffic light, symbolising the protagonist's journey through different stages of adjustment and acceptance in his new environment. The story alternates between Old Mak's current life in Hong Kong and the life he left behind in the village in China, providing ample opportunities for the exploration of the past perfect which conveys 'the past of the past'.

Said began by having students read the text, engage in discussions and annotate the series of events. The key highlight was Said's emphasis on the past perfect to illustrate clarity in the sequence of events. He skilfully guided students in discovering grammatical nuances, asking questions that prompted them to consider the significance of the use of the past perfect over the use of the simple past. As Said brought up in the interview:

> [The students] could see that the past perfect was used but at the same time, there was also the simple past tense there . . . so they were trying to uncover that portion. And at that point in time, I could see them figuring out how the word 'had' was significant – that was an 'aha!' moment.

Through verbal discussions and a subsequent Padlet activity, Said ensured active student engagement. The Padlet exercise involved extracting sentences from the text, encouraging students to discuss and analyse how the past perfect was used to convey a particular event in the story.

The following is the excerpt from 'Red, Amber, Green' which Said used (the past perfect forms have been underlined).

EXCERPT 4.10

> *Old Mak sighed, shut his eyes and rested his head against the wall. His close cropped hair, cut almost like that of a bonze, contained a liberal scattering of grey. Although he <u>had spent</u> so many years in the city he <u>had</u> not yet <u>learned</u> to mask his feelings. His simple peasant face displayed bewilderment for all the world to see. His sad drooping eyes, his broad flat nose and his apologetic mouth all confessed his helplessness and despair.*
>
> *He reflected upon the woes that <u>had befallen</u> him one after another and the circumstances that <u>had brought</u> him to Hong Kong. It seemed his whole life <u>had been</u> one long chronicle of woes. They began in the year of the great drought, when his two sisters had to be sold to a fate he <u>had</u> never quite <u>discovered</u>. A couple of years later a typhoon <u>had devastated</u> the village and <u>had killed</u> many people, including his father. The funeral expenses, coupled with the loss of the crops, <u>had forced</u> the sale of the small family plot. Thereafter he and his mother <u>had had</u> to work as casual farm hands. When he was eighteen his mother also died and nothing remained thereafter to bind him to the village.*

In the application phase, Said transitioned his students from understanding the past perfect in texts to applying it within their own narrative compositions – with a special emphasis on role models. He guided them through discussions on how employing the past perfect could enhance the clarity and coherence of their narratives. Through prompts, students were encouraged to integrate the past perfect into their writing, emphasising the portrayal of sequential events and reflective insights. Said provided feedback and support as students experimented with incorporating the past perfect forms into their narratives, fostering a deeper understanding of its usage and significance in their writing endeavours.

In all, Said felt that the lessons were effective, as seen in the evidence in the writing produced by his students: 'It was successful because at the end of the day, students understood how the past perfect was used in the text. This will enable them to use the past perfect more purposefully for meaning making' (Said's reflections)

Extracts Used in Chapter 4

The following is the extract from *The Amazing Komodo Dragon*, written by Fitri Kurniawan.

'Hurray! Uncle Benny is coming to visit us!' Maida said while waving the postcard she just received from the postman. 'And what is more exciting is that Uncle will take us all for holiday. Anywhere we like!' She yelled again.

'Let's go abroad! They have a lot of sales now!' Kak Neni shouted from her room. 'What if we go to Komodo Island?' Dad suggested. He was apparently watching a TV program about Komodo dragons.

'Oh no! It must be dirty and smelly there. Besides, there are a lot of dinosaurs just everywhere! Gee!' Kak Neni shuddered. 'The Komodo dragon is not a dinosaur, although they also have existed since the prehistoric time,' Maida explained imitating Mr. Sofyan, her Biology teacher.

'Let's vote! The place with most votes wins!' Kak Neni said confidently. 'Shopping somewhere overseas!' Kak Neni said while raising her hand up in the air.

Dad, Mom, and Kak Berlian looked (sensing) at one another. 'What! Nobody wants to go abroad?' Kak Neni yelled disappointedly. 'Going to Komodo Island should be nice, Nen. Indonesia is the only country with Komodo dragons. How can we only watch them on TV!' Kak Berlian said. 'OK! Komodo Island, here we come!' Kak Neni said sulkily.

The following is the extract from the story 'The Island' (pp. 169–171), in *Kebaya Tales*, written by Lee Su Kim (saying verbs are underlined).

'No pork. Anybody here got bring pork? Tolong buang. Throw away. Or else I not going to the island. And you not going too,' the boatman <u>reminded</u> us one more time before we boarded the boat for Pulau Besar.

'*Jangan main-main*,' he <u>warned</u>, 'the spirits on Pulau Besar are powerful.'

My twin brothers were dancing about on the jetty, dressed in their spanking new branded outdoor gear, their baseball caps worn back to front. Their rhythmic jerky movements weren't exactly inspired by extreme excitement or anything like that; rather, it was because of the trance music from those thingies perpetually stuck in their ears.

'Hey, did you two hear what he said?' I <u>snapped</u> at them and tried to pull the ear plugs out of the twin standing next to me. He ducked and stuck out a reddish, sugar-coated tongue at me.

Mum <u>scolded</u>, 'Cindy, leave them alone. Let them enjoy themselves.'

The twins grinned irritatingly and continued bobbing along with the throbbing din from their MP3 players, heads nodding, bodies twitching perpetually. They were eleven years old, just five years younger than me, but we were so completely different. I love history, nature and books. They were the opposite – they never read at all, loathed history or anything older than ten days. They would start sweating within minutes if the air was not 'conditioned'. Their idea of a perfect day was chatting to cyberspace friends on their PCs and playing computer games till the cows come home.

When Dad told us about this trip, they responded with their usual 'enthusiasm' whenever it meant going into the outdoors.

'Awwww, must we? An island? Ewww, how boring,' said Damien.

'How long does it take to get there? Where is it? What? In Malacca? You mean we have to go all the way to Malacca? Uggh, why can't we stay at home?' said Brendan.

'Oh quit complaining. You've never ever been to an island before,' I told them. 'Come to think of it, you've never been anywhere remotely close to nature!'

Damien and Brendan immediately ganged up on me.

'Who sez so? I've been to the pyramids of Egypt and the ruins of Angkor,' Damien the smart aleck <u>shot back</u>.

'Yeah, I've shot savages from my jet plane! And bomb terrorists in the deserts!' Brendan <u>retorted</u>.

'In front of the PC without moving your lazy bums? Yeah, right,' I <u>scoffed</u>.

'And by the way, pyramids are manmade, stupid,' I <u>added</u> sarcastically. 'Do you guys even know what nature means?'

'Nature? Nature means hot, sticky and sweaty. Yechh! Hey, Sis, are you sure you want to go to this island? Think of the mozzies! No toilet . . . you will have to dig a hole or do it in the lalang . . . yucckk . . . think of the leeches coming for you, Ha ha ha!' Brendan <u>teased</u> me.

Damien <u>whined</u>, 'An island, Dad? Awww, who needs to go to an island Dad? I can just google it for you. It's like the real thing. Virtual island, no sweat. Save on petrol, Dad.'

The following is the extract from the story 'Red, Amber, Green' (pp. 2–3), in *Collected Hong Kong Stories*, written by David T.K. Wong.

It has been a long, long time since he witnessed the breaking of the dawn, Old Mak thought, as he watched the sky turning a light translucent blue. The cubicle in the lodging-house, where he had occupied for years one layer of a three-tiered bunk, was windowless. Day and night were only distinguishable, except for the comings and goings of the other occupants of the cubicle as they went about their shifts as coolies, street sweepers, night watchmen or whatever. In the police cell there was at least sunlight. 'They squeeze you till there's no way out, those lackeys of foreign devils,' the young man said, with a note of righteous complaint in his voice. 'If you cannot afford to line their pockets, you cannot get a licence. If you sell without a licence, you're breaking the law. Then they put you in gaol and confiscate your goods. How is a man to live?' Old Mak turned towards the young man. He noticed that he had long ears, with large fleshy lobes, just like his own. To the Chinese long ears were supposed to mean longevity, and he wondered if the young man ever found any pleasure in the thought. He himself had once. But that was forty years ago, when he first came to Hong Kong, when he was filled with hope of crossing the seas to the Golden Mountain to earn enough money to buy back the family land. Now, worn out, kinless and without hope, a long life seemed a cruel and unnecessary burden. Old Mak sighed, shut his eyes and rested his head against the wall. His close cropped hair, cut almost like that of a bonze, contained a liberal scattering of grey. Although he had spent so many years in the city he had not yet learned to mask his feelings. His simple peasant face displayed bewilderment for all the world to see. His sad drooping eyes, his broad flat nose and his apologetic mouth all confessed his helplessness and despair. He reflected upon the woes that had befallen him one after another and the circumstances that had brought him to Hong Kong. It seemed his whole life had been one long chronicle of woes. They began in the year of the great drought, when his two sisters had to be sold to a fate he had never quite discovered. A couple of years later a typhoon had devastated the village and had killed many people, including his father. The funeral expenses, coupled with the loss of the crops, had forced the sale of the small family plot. Thereafter he and his mother had had to work as casual farm hands. When he was eighteen his mother also died and nothing remained thereafter to bind him to the village.

References

Alsagoff, L. (2023). *A Visual Guide to English Grammar*. Marshall Cavendish.
Kurniawan, F. (2016). *The Amazing Komodo Dragon*. Gramedia Publishing Company.
Lee, S.K. (2011). The island. In *Kebaya Tales*. Marshall Cavendish.
Wong, D.T.K. (1996). Red, amber, green. In *Collected Hong Kong Stories*. Blacksmith Books.

5 Clauses and Sentences

What Are Clauses?

The verb phrase is the most important element in a clause. As such, clauses describe events or states as they are built from verb phrases. The number of clauses in a sentence may be determined by counting the number of verb phrases present in the sentence. For example, there is one clause in *The brown, skinny dog ate the food hungrily*, as there is one verb phrase *ate*, two clauses in *Stop shouting!*, as there are two verb phrases *stop* and *shouting* and three clauses in *While Lili was running in the park, she slipped on a banana peel and fell on her back*, as there are three different verb phrases, *was running*, *slipped* and *fell*.

Types of Clauses

There are two main types of clauses – a main (or independent) clause and a subordinate (or dependent) clause. A **main clause** can stand alone independently. It must be a finite clause that contains not only a finite verb phrase, but also an explicit subject. For example, in the following sentence, the finite verb phrase is *carried* and the explicit subject is *Paul*:

> *Paul carried his black leather briefcase to work.*

There are two exceptions, though, to this rule. The first exception is that in an imperative sentence, the main or the standalone clause is a non-finite clause that comprises a non-finite verb phrase like in *Come in!*, where the verb phrase *come* is in its base form. The other exception is when main clauses are coordinated with coordinating conjunctions like *and* and *but*, and have a shared subject. The subject in the second coordinated main clause may be ellipted to avoid repetition. Here is an example where the repeated subject is placed in brackets to indicate that it is optional to mention it:

> *Minju baked some chocolate chip cookies and (Minju) gave them to her friends for Christmas.*

DOI: 10.4324/9781003255963-5

A **subordinate clause**, on the other hand, cannot stand alone independently. It must either be attached to a main clause, or be embedded in larger clauses or phrases, like in a noun phrase. A subordinate clause may be a finite clause with a finite verb phrase or a non-finite clause with a non-finite verb phrase and may or may not have explicit subjects. Examples of subordinate clauses in relation to main clauses are below (subordinate clauses are underlined and verb phrases in the subordinate clauses are bolded):

<u>When the bell **rang**,</u> the students ran to the field.

(Subordinate clause starting with a subordinating conjunction *when* which contains a finite verb phrase *rang*, attached to the main clause *the students ran to the field*.)

It was announced <u>that Maria **aced** the examinations.</u>

(Subordinate clause starting with a subordinating conjunction *that* which contains a finite verb phrase *aced*, embedded in the main clause *It was announced X*, where X is the subordinate clause *that Maria aced the examinations*.)

<u>**Feeling** upset,</u> Ella slammed the door.

(Subordinate clause starting with a non-finite *-ing* verb phrase *feeling*, attached to the main clause *Ella slammed the door*.)

The pianist wants <u>**to perform** with the choir</u>

(Subordinate clause starting with a non-finite *to*-infinitive verb phrase *to perform*, embedded in the main clause *The pianist wants X*, where X is the subordinate clause *to perform with the choir*.)

The man <u>who **is wearing** the blue tie</u> looks highly suspicious.

(Subordinate clause starting with a relative pronoun *who* containing a finite verb phrase *is wearing* is embedded as the postmodifier of the head noun *man* in the noun phrase *the man who is wearing the blue tie*. This noun phrase is the subject, X, of the main clause *X looks highly suspicious*.)

I do not know <u>how the fire **started**</u>.

(Subordinate clause starting with a wh-word *how* containing a finite verb phrase *started*, embedded in the main clause *I do not know X* where X is the subordinate clause *how the fire started*.)

From the analysis of the examples above, you will note that there are various ways to start a subordinate clause. Some of these ways are the following:

- Starting with a subordinating conjunction (examples include *while, since, because, although*).
- Starting with a non-finite verb (these include the *-ing* clauses and the infinitive clauses that begin with the bare or *to-*infinitive verbs).
- Starting with a relative pronoun or relative adverb (examples include *which, that, whom, where*).
- Starting with a *wh-*word (examples include *what, why, how*).

Combining Clauses

There are two main ways in which we can combine clauses – coordination and subordination. Let's start with **coordination**. The process of coordination joins main clauses together. Here, there is a relationship between a main clause and a main clause. Main clauses are joined together with either coordinating conjunctions or conjunctive adverbs. Examples of coordinating conjunctions are the following:

for, and, neither . . . nor (or *either . . . or*), *but, or, yet* and *so*

(Note: recall in Chapter 2, that a common acronym by which coordinating conjunctions are remembered is FANBOYS, as indicated by the first letter of the coordinating conjunctions listed here.)

Coordinating conjunctions used to coordinate main clauses carry different meanings. For example:

- *and* – to add on main ideas
- *but, yet* – to contrast main ideas
- *or, either . . . or* – to offer alternatives or choices of main ideas

Conjunctive adverbs are adverbs that behave like conjunctions. Examples of conjunctive adverbs are the following:

nevertheless, however, consequently, next, then, hence, therefore, in comparison

These conjunctive adverbs also carry different meanings. For example:

- *moreover, furthermore* – to add an extra piece of information
- *next, then* – to add another element in a list
- *thus, therefore, hence* – expressing a result
- *meanwhile, meantime* – shifting attention to a simultaneous action

Examples of main clauses (underlined) being joined together through coordination are the following (coordinating conjunctions are bolded):

Tia swept the floor **and** *moped it clean*. (to signal an addition of ideas)
Mark is good at drawing **but** *he is bad at painting.* (to signal a contrast of ideas)
She applied for the job; **however,** *she did not have the qualifications for it.* (to also signal a contrast of ideas)

The process of **subordination** involves the attaching or joining of a subordinate clause to a main clause or the embedding of a subordinate clause in another larger clause or phrase. Here there is a relationship between a main clause and one or more subordinate clauses (note: subordinate clauses may be formed in various ways as mentioned above). Examples of subordinate clauses in relation to main clauses are the following (subordinate clauses are underlined and starting words of subordinate clauses bolded):

While *skipping to the playground,* the children sang happy songs.
Carrying *a heavy pile of books,* the little girl stumbled.
I gave my mother a hug for the cake **which** *she lovingly baked for me.*

Subordination is usually created using subordinating conjunctions as those mentioned above. Like coordinating conjunctions and conjunctive adverbs, subordinating conjunctions used to introduce subordinate clauses also carry different meanings. For example:

- *because, since* – to introduce a subordinate clause that provides a reason or cause for what is stated in the main clause
- *if, unless* – to introduce a subordinate clause that states a condition related to the outcome in the main clause.
- *when, while, before* – to introduce a time-related subordinate clause connected to the action in the main clause.

What Are Sentences?

Types of Sentences

There are four types of sentences. The number of clauses, the types of clauses and how these clauses are joined (or related) determine the types of sentences formed. There are essentially four types of sentences. These are simple, compound, complex and compound-complex sentences. The different types of sentences are elaborated on below.

Simple Sentence

Simple sentences are made up of one clause. As we mentioned earlier, a clause is essentially made up of a verb phrase, and verb phrases express actions or states of being. We can think of actions or states of being as ideas. By extension then, a simple sentence, which is made up of one clause, carries one idea. This clause must be a main clause as only a main clause can be independent and stand alone. As such, a simple sentence is made up of one main clause, and hence, a main idea. Examples of simple sentences are as follows (verb phrases are underlined):

> Tanya <u>read</u> the entire book in a day.
> The chicken <u>was roasted</u> in that oven.
> <u>Did</u> the team <u>win</u> at the SEA Games?

Compound Sentence

Compound sentences are created through the process of coordination. Coordination involves the joining together of two or more main clauses that are grammatical equal. This means that compound sentences are made up of two or more main ideas that are of equal importance. The choice of coordinating conjunctions or conjunctive adverbs used to join these two or more main clauses will determine the relationship between these clauses. For example, these two main clauses *Alif is rich* and *Alif is generous*, which can stand alone as two independent clauses, may be joined together with either the coordinating conjunction *and* or *but*, as in the following:

> Alif <u>is</u> rich **and** he <u>is</u> generous.
> Alif <u>is</u> rich **but** he <u>is</u> generous.

However, these two compound sentences do not mean the same. In using the coordinating conjunction *and*, the idea that Alif is generous is added on to the idea that Alif is rich. The attribute of being generous is added on to the attribute of Alif being rich. However, in using the coordinating conjunction *but*, the attribute of being generous is contrasted to the attribute of being rich. There is the assumption conveyed here that rich people are not usually generous, but in this case, Alif is quite the exception – he is rich but he is generous. The two main ideas are contrasted. As such, the choice in the use of different coordinating conjunctions results in the expression of two different meanings. Other examples of compound sentences with the use of conjunctive adverbs are as follows (verb phrases, and hence ideas, are underlined and the conjunctive adverbs are bolded):

> Haris <u>did</u> not <u>study</u> for his examination; **consequently**, he <u>failed</u> it.
> There <u>was</u> a power outage; **hence**, the lifts <u>are</u> not <u>working</u>.

Complex Sentence

Complex sentences are created through the process of subordination. Subordination involves the joining of a main clause and one or more subordinate clauses. The main clause carries the main idea, while the subordinate clauses carry the supporting or additional ideas to the main clause. As such, the clauses, and hence, ideas are not grammatically equal. Main ideas can stand alone, while supporting ideas cannot stand alone. For example, in the complex sentence below (verb phrases are underlined)

While the sun <u>was shining</u> brightly, the children <u>swam</u> happily in the river.

the main clause is *the children swam happily in the river*. This is the main idea of the sentence. The subordinate clause *while the sun was shining brightly*, adds additional information to the main idea. You will note that this supporting idea cannot stand alone.

Other examples of complex sentences are as follows (main clauses are bolded and subordinate clauses are underlined):

Felicia made a ham sandwich <u>because she was feeling famished.</u>

(Subordinate clause is the supporting idea giving the reason for the action in the main clause.)

I asked Tsui Fen <u>what time she would be arriving that night.</u>

(Main clause structure is *I asked Tsui Fen X* where X is the subordinate clause *what time she would be arriving that night* that gives additional information.)

Our grandfather taught us many lessons which helped us in life.

(Subordinate clause *which helped us in life* is a postmodifier of the head noun *lessons* in the noun phrase *many lessons which helped us in life*, which is the direct object, X, of the main clause *Our grandfather taught us X.*)

Compound-Complex Sentence

Compound-complex sentences are created through a combination of coordination (compound sentences) with subordination (complex sentences). Unlike complex sentences which contain only one main clause and one or more subordinate clauses, a compound-complex sentence may contain more than one main clause and one or more subordinate clauses (that is, may contain more than one main idea and one or more supporting or additional ideas). Here are some examples of compound-complex sentences (subordinate clauses which create the complex structures are underlined and coordinating conjunctions or conjunctive adverbs that create the compound structures are bolded). Do note that the combination of coordination and subordination in compound-complex sentences may play out in various ways:

> Ronnie enjoys <u>singing in the school choir</u>; **however**, he does not like <u>performing on stage</u>.

(Two complex sentences joined together with the conjunctive adverb *however*.)

> <u>While running on the wet pavement</u>, he fell **and** twisted his ankle.

(A subordinate clause joined to a compound sentence *he fell and twisted his ankle*.)

> Kieren was late for work <u>because he woke up late **and** missed the bus</u>.

(Subordinate clauses to the main clause *Kieren was late for work* are coordinated with the coordinating conjunction *and*.)

The choice of which types of clauses and sentences to use in crafting a spoken or written text will depend on several factors like the purpose, audience, context or culture of the specific text. Usually, a variety of types of sentences (simple, compound, complex and compound-complex) are used in a narrative to convey different relationships between ideas expressed and to create impact. This point will be illustrated through the analyses of excerpts from the narrative *Where's Grandma?* in the next section.

Clauses and Sentences as Meaning Making in Texts

This narrative is largely written using complex and compound-complex sentences where there is the linking of main clauses and subordinate clauses in various ways. This means that the main ideas in the narrative are usually joined by subordinating ideas that support or elaborate on the main ideas.

In the analyses of the sentences below in the selected excerpts from the opening chapter of the narrative, simple sentences are labelled S, complex sentences are labelled CX and compound-complex sentences are labelled CP-CX. There are no compound sentences in the selected excerpts. In the analyses, the subordinate clauses are underlined and coordinating conjunctions that signal compound sentences (in compound-complex sentences) are bolded.

EXCERPT 5.1

> <u>When I was little</u>, Grandma took me to the nearby playground every evening (CX). She would hold my hand <u>as we walked through the void decks and car parks</u> (CX).
> <u>When we approached the playground</u>, I would dash to the swings **and** then feel Grandma's warm palms <u>pushing my back</u> <u>as I soared into the sky</u> (CP-CX).

EXCERPT 5.2

> *Grandma would also be around <u>to help</u> <u>when I fell</u>* (CX). *She would check <u>if I was alright</u> and encourage me <u>to get up on my feet</u>* (CP-CX). *<u>If there was a wound</u>, she would quickly take out her handkerchief <u>to wipe away the blood</u>* (CX).

As mentioned earlier, the use of complex and compound-complex sentences conveys different relationships between ideas, specifically the relationship between main and subordinating ideas, where the subordinating ideas support or elaborate on the main ideas, as in the complex and compound-complex sentences analysed in the excerpts.

Given that this narrative is about Grandma who used to be healthy and active, but then suffers the onset of Alzheimer's disease that is triggered by a fall, the narrative moves back and forth in time to compare healthy Grandma and ill Grandma. As such, for example, the subordinate conjunction *when* to signal time is used to create the subordinate clause *When I was little* in the complex sentence *When I was little, Grandma took me to the nearby playground every evening* to signal a shift back in time when Luke was little, and Grandma was healthy and could take Luke to the playground every evening. The main idea is that Grandma was once healthy and fit but the subordinate clause adds important information that this was only the case when Luke was little. Another example is the use of the subordinate clause *when I fell* in the complex sentence *Grandma would also be around to help when I fell* to signal once again a shift back in time when Grandma used to help Luke when Luke was the one who fell (in contrast to the time when it was Grandma who fell). The subordinate clauses used here add important information to the main ideas to contrast healthy Grandma and ill Grandma.

Other subordinate conjunctions to convey time like *as* and *while* are also used to create subordinate clauses that add more information to when a main idea was carried out. For example, the subordinate clause *as we walked through the void decks and car parks* adds to when Grandma would hold Luke's hand in Excerpt 5.1. Again, this subordinate clause adds information to suggest that in the past, Grandma was strong – strong enough to walk long distances and she was the one guiding Luke.

Apart from the use of subordinating conjunctions that signal time, there is the use of the subordinating conjunction *if* to signal the conditional in the narrative, as seen in Excerpt 5.2. The subordinate clauses that start with the subordinating conjunction *if* in the compound-complex sentence *She would check <u>if I was alright</u> and encourage me to get up on my feet* and the complex sentence *<u>If there was a wound</u>, she would quickly take out her handkerchief to wipe away the blood* elaborate on the main ideas expressed that Grandma was very loving and caring towards Luke before her Alzheimer's disease (that is, she would check on Luke and she would wipe away blood on Luke if needed).

Besides the use of subordinate clauses starting with subordinating conjunctions, there are also subordinate clauses used in the excerpts starting with non-finite verbs, and hence are non-finite clauses. For example, the non-finite subordinate clause *to wipe away the blood* in Excerpt 5.2 elaborates on why Grandma would take her handkerchief out (the main idea).

As illustrated through the analyses, subordinate clauses, though they do not convey main ideas, play an important role in the development of a narrative, in supporting and adding on to the main ideas in a narrative to help in the flow and storyline of the narrative. We will learn in Chapter 6 that in many instances, subordinate clauses play the role of adverbials in a text. Adverbials answer questions of when, where, why and how of the main verb (in the main clause) and hence elaborate and support the main clauses. Most of the subordinate causes highlighted in the excerpts above hence play the role of adverbials.

When there are simple sentences used in the narrative, they seem to be concentrated within specific paragraphs as seen in the excerpt below:

EXCERPT 5.3

> *Things changed after the fall* (S). *It was Grandma <u>who fell</u>* (CX). <u>*While coming out of the toilet,*</u> *Grandma slipped* **and** *crashed onto the floor* (CP-CX). *Kaboonk!*
>
> *I dashed to the toilet* (S). *Grandma was groaning softly* (S). *Blood oozed from a deep gash on her forehead* (S). *She had also sprained her left ankle* (S). *That happened almost two months ago* (S). <u>*Although Grandma recovered,*</u> *she walks with a slight limp and a walking stick* (CX).
>
> *Grandma's fall was just the beginning* (S).

The purpose of the simple sentences as used in Excerpt 5.3 is to create impact. As mentioned earlier, the turning point (that is, the complication) of the narrative is when Grandma fell. The concentration of simple sentences in the second paragraph of Excerpt 5.3 focuses on the time when Grandma fell. One main idea is listed after another (verb phrases and hence, actions are underlined) – *I* (Luke) <u>*dashed*</u> *to the toilet; Grandma <u>was groaning</u> softly; Blood <u>oozed</u> from a deep gash on her forehead; She <u>had</u> also <u>sprained</u> her ankle*. The main ideas listed one after another in this paragraph paint this vivid picture of the moment Grandma fell. And as stated in the simple sentence at the start of Excerpt 5.3, *Things <u>changed</u> after the fall*.

It is important to note that every sentence type has its place in the crafting of a piece of text. A simple sentence does not mean it is less in significance or complexity (in terms of meaning) than a complex sentence. A simple sentence may be the most impactful in terms of meaning, as highlighted in the analysis above. Each type of sentence has its role to play in the creation of a piece of text, in how ideas are put together and in how relationships between and amongst ideas are created.

The choice of types of sentences to use will depend on the purpose, audience, context and culture of a text. Here, it is important to revisit our discussion of noun phrases used in the narrative in Chapter 3. In Chapter 3, we discussed that the narrative largely uses simple noun phrases, likely to attend to the target audience of the narrative which is a younger audience. However, given that this is a narrative that moves back and forth in time to compare healthy Grandma in the past, and ill Grandma after the fall, it is critical to introduce details and information in subordinate clauses that will support and guide young readers to move back and forth in this storyline. As such, there is the use of more complex and compound-complex sentences in this narrative. The use of simple noun phrases then balances the complexity of grammatical structures used in this narrative to consider the needs of the target audience.

Exploring Sentence Types with 11- and 12-Year-Olds

In this section, we will be introduced to a unit of work designed by HingMH and Felice. Both teachers work in the same school as Gajen (see Chapter 3). HingMH and Felice decided that they would co-construct the lessons but would enact the lessons for different profiles of learners. Felice's students were 11-year-old middle-readiness learners and HingMH ones were 12-year-olds and of low readiness. The teachers enacted the unit through an exploration of grammar as a resource for conveying meaning, with a specific focus on various sentence types. The objective was to highlight the direct relationship between sentence types and the nuanced expression of ideas. The teachers observed that their students' writing lacked sentence variety, that is, they frequently used simple sentences and on occasion when they used compound sentences, they often relied on common conjunctions, such as *and* and *so*. Additionally, their written pieces often contained awkward structures with multiple ideas crammed into run-on sentences.

Felice and HingMH intentionally chose authentic Asian texts because they felt that these were contextually more familiar to their learners. They also chose texts that contained the range of sentence types needed for them to demonstrate how they were used within authentic situations. They scaffolded the grammar analyses, ensuring that students could comprehend and apply knowledge of sentence types effectively. By analysing simple, compound and complex sentences within the context of a text, their students were able to gain insights into how grammatical choices impacted the clarity and effectiveness of the expression of ideas within texts. These lessons were designed to provide a detailed and straightforward examination of the grammatical domain, allowing students to appreciate how writers made use of sentence types to achieve certain intended effects; and to also understand how sentence types contribute to purposeful expression in the students' own writing.

In this series of lessons, the teachers ensured that a wide range of literacy skills were seamlessly integrated. These included listening, viewing, reading, speaking, writing, and representing. HingMH in her interview emphasised that the lesson was not meant to be just about the final writing product. Instead, she found herself incorporating various language skills to ensure that there was meaning and relevance in what was taught. For instance, students engaged in activities such as reading aloud their own written pieces which not only develops their writing and reading skills but also enhances their oral communication abilities.

HingMH explained:

> The end product is the writing, but as I was teaching the lesson, I found myself having to weave in various language skills for this lesson to be meaningful. As I thought deeper, it actually helps the students to see the lesson as a meaningful whole rather than seeing the language features in isolation.
>
> (HingMH, Interview)

This comprehensive approach underscores the power of contextualised grammar teaching, which allows students to experience language learning as an integrated and meaningful process. By deliberating developing all these skills within a unit, learners can see how different aspects of language work together, resulting in a more enriched overall literacy development.

HingMH and Felice chose to work with two authentic Asian texts – the first was a Filipino song, 'Basang-Basa sa Ulan', and the other a short story, 'Lyca Gairanod: Thank you, Jesus' by writer and educator, Carmelita Ballesteros. Both texts are linked by a similar theme of resilience.

'Basang-Basa sa Ulan' is a song that captures the universal themes of heartbreak and resilience. It conveys the message that even in our most challenging times, we have the strength to rise and keep moving forward. The song illustrates that healing and personal growth come from confronting our pain head-on rather than avoiding it. The song tells the story of a protagonist who feels alone and lost in the darkness, repeatedly stumbling and falling, yet demonstrating an unwavering resolve to get back up each time.

'Lyca Gairanod: Thank you, Jesus' tells the story of Lyca Gairanod, one of eight children from a poor family. Her father worked as a fisherman, and her mother collected recyclable plastics and bottles. The family lived in very adverse conditions. Despite her small frame and fragile appearance, nine-year-old Lyca showed remarkable strength. She rose to fame as the first grand champion of *The Voice Kids Philippines* in 2014. Her prize was a house, one million pesos in cash and another million pesos in a trust fund. Her story is an inspiring one and a testament to resilience and gratitude in the face of great adversity.

The unit which Felice and HingMH designed comprised eight lessons – one building on another which eventually culminated in a writing activity. The following is a simple schematic of their lesson flow.

Lesson 1: Song and Reading of Authentic Text for Enjoyment

- To set the context, students listen to Filipino song 'Basang-Basa sa Ulan'.
  - Discuss the song's meaning and relevance to the upcoming text.
- Students are introduced to the text 'Lyca Gairanod: Thank you, Jesus' for reading.
  - Discuss key points about Lyca's life and challenges.
  - Connect the text to the value of resilience.

Lesson 2: Identifying and Analysing Simple Sentences (S)

- Activity (simple sentences)
  - Analyse and identify characteristics of simple sentences from the authentic text 'Lyca Gairanod: Thank you, Jesus'.

Lesson 3: Identifying and Analysing Compound Sentences (CP)

- Activity (compound sentences)
  - Analyse and identify characteristics of compound sentences.
  - Compare simple and compound sentences.
  - Discuss the use and impact of different sentence types in the text.

Lesson 4: Recapping Simple and Compound Sentences; Identifying and Analysing Complex Sentences (CX)

- Activity (complex sentences)
  - Analyse and identify characteristics of complex sentences in the authentic text.
  - Discuss the form and function of main and subordinate clauses.
  - Explicit teaching and application.

Lesson 5: Discussing Complex Sentences

- Ways of forming complex sentences
- Application
- Compare complex sentences with simple and compound sentences

Lesson 6: Listening Activity

- Compare two texts with different sentence types.

Lesson 7: Applying to Writing

- Use different sentence types to improve writing.

Lesson 8: Reading/Writing Activity

- Examine authentic Asian text with varied sentence types.
- Apply to writing (continue with drafting).

The series of lessons were originally planned to be enacted over 150 minutes (about 5 lessons). However, in HingMH's case, as her students were low readiness 12-year-olds, they were extended over two weeks (eight lessons) because she wanted to ensure a thorough understanding. The extra help and scaffolding she provided within each lesson helped her students connect the dots between sentence types and meaningful reading and writing.

The following are a few sample highlights from the grammar package the teachers produced.

Sample 1 (Lesson 4)

Simple Sentences
Underline the verbs/ verb phrases in each sentence.

1. *Lyca was one of eight children of a poor couple.*
2. *She and her family lived in a shack near the seashore of Tanza, Cavite, Philippines.*
3. *She was very strong.*
4. *She went to school irregularly.*

Compound Sentences (Pair Work)
Underline the verbs/ verb phrases in each sentence.

1. *She'd go around the gated, residential villages and she'd collect plastics and bottles.*
2. *She'd be very happy with thirty pesos and she'd buy half a kilo of rice and dried fish.*
3. *Her favourite band was Aegis and her favourite songs were 'Halik' and 'Narito Ako'.*

The purpose of the activities in Sample 1 was for the teachers to engage their students in recognising and understanding the structures of simple and compound sentences. In the first part, students underlined verb phrases in simple sentences that described Lyca's life (the text which they encountered earlier). This encouraged them to grasp the basic components of straightforward sentence construction, and that simple sentences convey one main idea. In the compound sentence exercise, students identified the two or more verb phrases that are contained in the sentence, conjoined using coordinating conjunctions. This emphasised the structure of compound sentences and how they involve the coordination of distinct ideas. Through these activities, students also learnt that verb phrases can represent different actions or states or ideas. By focusing on the structure of sentences, the activity aimed to develop students' understanding of sentence types and their ability to recognise and hopefully construct sentences with different complexities.

Sample 2 (Lesson 5)

Text A (adapted)	Text B (original)
• *Lyca went to school irregularly* (S). • *Sometimes, she would sneak out of school* (S). • *She would be too worried* (S). • *There was no food for a sick sibling at home* (S). • *She'd go around the gated, residential villages* (S). • *She'd collect plastics and bottles* (S). • *Then she'd sell her meagre collection to a junk yard operator* (S). • *She'd be very happy with thirty pesos* (S). • *She'd buy half a kilo of rice and dried fish* (S).	• *Lyca went to school irregularly* (S). • *Sometimes, she would sneak out of school because she'd be too worried that there was no food for a sick sibling at home* (CX). • *She'd go around the gated, residential villages and she'd collect plastics and bottles* (CP). • *Then she'd sell her meagre collection to a junk yard operator* (S). • *She'd be very happy with thirty pesos and she'd buy half a kilo of rice and dried fish* (CP).

Sample 2 was a simple yet effective task for students to understand sentence types and how they affect meaning. Students compared Text A which comprised only simple sentences with Text B which has a variety of sentence types. When read aloud, the students felt that Text A had too many stops and it was difficult to listen to and ascertain the meaning of the text. Text B, on the other hand, afforded easier listening as it did not have too many stops. The students also found it easier to understand and see the linking of ideas. The important lesson learnt with this activity is that varying sentence types significantly impacts the clarity, readability and overall effectiveness of a text. Through the reading aloud, students realised that incorporating different sentence structures can enhance the flow of reading (hence, writing), making it more engaging and easier to understand.

In all, the teachers felt that their students benefitted from this approach to teaching grammar. Felice found that this approach was beneficial in improving her students' writing skills, stating, 'Raising awareness was really good. Suddenly, grammar had a part to play in writing.' As HingMH put it succinctly in her interview, 'The whole idea is to help students understand the functions and the forms of these sentence types so that they can use different sentence types meaningfully in their writing . . . helps sequence their ideas.'

Through the interview, HingMH shared valuable insights into her personal learning as an educator. Notably, she embraced the use of mentor texts as a powerful tool for teaching grammar and leveraging such texts to enhance students' comprehension. This approach allowed her to creatively weave grammatical concepts into meaningful lessons, contributing to a deeper understanding among her students.

HingMH underscored the importance of continuous professional growth. Engaging in collaborative dialogues, co-teaching and co-planning with colleagues provided her with diverse perspectives and enriched her teaching strategies. Additionally, the experience prompted her to adopt intentional and strategic planning, emphasising the need to focus on one key idea per lesson. Her commitment to simplifying explanations, incorporating relatable terms and imagery reflected a dedication to ensuring her students could grasp grammatical concepts effectively. In a separate interview, Felice's views were very much aligned with HingMH's. She expressed that lesson planning becomes more effective and analytical when working with a partner. Felice also noted that having a collaborative approach allows for the exchange of ideas and perspectives. Like HingMH, Felice highlighted a shift in her perspective on teaching writing, recognising the newfound importance of grammar as a crucial element of meaning making in composition.

The teachers also expressed a strong belief in the importance of incorporating Asian texts into the curriculum, emphasising their value in providing diverse linguistic perspectives and cultural insights. HingMH saw these texts as rich resources for exploring grammatical structures and linguistic nuances, contributing to a more comprehensive understanding of language. Felice shared that Asian-origin stories were more relatable and easier for her students to understand, given their age and lack of travel experiences. Both teachers strongly felt a commitment to cultural inclusivity in education, aiming to create an environment where students can connect with the content on a personal and meaningful level, ultimately enhancing their engagement with language learning.

Extract Used in Chapter 5

The following is the extract from 'Lyca Gairanod: Thank you, Jesus' (pp. 1–2), written by Carmelita C. Ballesteros.

> *Who was she? Lyca was one of eight children of a poor couple. Her father was a small-time fisherman while her mother was a junk collector of recyclable plastics and bottles. She and her family lived in a shack near the seashore of Tanza, Cavite, Philippines.*
>
> *To help put food on the table, Lyca collected junk with her mother and siblings. You see, fishing did not always yield a good catch. During stormy weather, there would be no catch at all. Only nine years old, Lyca was petite and fragile. But she was not weak. She was very strong. She was like the boy David who slew the giant Goliath.*
>
> *'Magbobote!' some of Lyca's school mates called her derisively. It was a form of verbal bullying. Her school mates were telling her that her 'occupation' was an anomaly among well-scrubbed kids whose parents were probably office employees.*

Lyca probably didn't take a bath every day. Who knows if she even brushed her teeth three times a day? If there was no money for a meal, why would she worry about brushing her teeth and taking a bath? She probably smelled.

Lyca went to school irregularly. Sometimes, she would sneak out of school because she'd be too worried that there was no food for a sick sibling at home. She'd go around the gated, residential villages and she'd collect plastics and bottles Then she'd sell her meager collection to a junk yard operator. She'd be very happy with thirty pesos and she'd buy half a kilo of rice and dried fish. She promised her family that one day, she'd win in a singing competition and she'd buy plenty of rice for all of them.

Lyca was a gifted child. Maybe she was an angel from heaven. She knew that she could sing well and she loved singing. Her rehearsal halls were the garbage pile near the sea, the streets, and the junk yard. Her audiences were neighbors who gave her a few pesos or some snack food.

Her voice coach was the radio. Her favorite band was Aegis and her favorite songs were 'Halik' and 'Narito Ako' (music and lyrics by Celso Abenoja and Nonong Pedero, respectively).

Reference

Ballesteros, C.C. (2014). Lyca Gairanod: Thank you, Jesus. *The FilAm MegaScene.* https://legacy1.filammegascene.com/?p=11205

6 Grammatical Functions

Form and Function

Chapters 2 to 5 looked at grammar as form. We now move on to looking at grammar as function. Form refers to the structures of words, phrases, clauses and sentences. When we discuss word class (e.g., nouns, verbs, prepositions and conjunctions), types of phrases (e.g., noun phrases, preposition phrases and adverb phrases), types of clauses (e.g., finite clauses and non-finite clauses) and types of sentences (e.g., simple sentences and complex sentences), we are discussing form. Function, on the other hand, refers to what roles these forms or structures play within context, that is, what words, phrases or clauses are doing in particular positions and in relation to each other in a sentence. Grammatical functional terms are subject, verb (distinguished from verb as a word class), object, complement and adverbial. Other grammatical functional terms that have been introduced in earlier chapters include premodifier, postmodifier and head (for example, of a noun phrase). Understanding and making this distinction in grammar between form and function is important for us to understand how language works, especially when we wish to understand how different forms can play different functions in language use. This knowledge and understanding will help us make grammatical choices of grammatical structures when expressing meaning in language use.

Clause Patterns and Transitivity

Before we can discuss the different grammatical functions, we must first understand clause patterns. In the previous chapter, we said that the most essential element or constituent of a clause is the verb phrase. The main or lexical verb of the verb phrase (that is, the process) determines the structure/pattern of the clause in terms of the types of participants that make up the clause. The type of main or lexical verb (V), for example, whether transitive or intransitive, will determine the number and types of obligatory or required participants. The types of required participants are subject (S), object (O) [objects can be either direct object (Od) and indirect object (Oi)] and complement (C) [complements can be either subject complement (Cs) or object complement (Co)].

DOI: 10.4324/9781003255963-6

There are generally five categories of verbs when we analyse verbs for transitivity. They are intransitive verbs, transitive verbs, linking (including copula), ditransitive verbs and complex-transitive verbs.

Intransitive Verbs (Verbs that Require Only One Participant)

Intransitive verbs require only one participant. This participant is a subject, and typically, the clause pattern here will be S + V. The following are examples of main or lexical verbs behaving as intransitive verbs:

The baby	is crawling.
S	V

The birds	soared.
S	V

The crowd	cheers.
S	V

Transitive Verbs (Verbs that Require Two Participants)

Transitive verbs require two participants. The participants are subject and object (by default the direct object here). Typically, the clause pattern here will be S + V + O. The following are examples of main or lexical verbs behaving as transitive verbs:

My mother	sliced	the cake.
S	V	O

The volunteers	are building	a playground.
S	V	O

Ximin	blew	all the candles.
S	V	O

Linking or Copula Verbs (Verbs that Require Two Participants)

Linking (including copula) verbs require two participants. The participants are subject and subject complement. Typically, the clause pattern here will be

S + V + Cs. Linking verbs essentially equate the subject to the subject complement. The following are examples of main or lexical verbs behaving as linking verbs:

The children	are	very excited.
S	V	Cs

Rajiv	became	the chairperson of the committee.
S	V	Cs

The school principal	seems	very kind.
S	V	Cs

Ditransitive Verbs (Verbs that Require Three Participants)

Ditransitive verbs require three participants. The participants are subject, direct object and indirect object. Ditransitive verbs typically allow for two clause patterns – S + V + Oi + Od or S + V + Od + Oi (here, if the Od comes first, the Oi will take the form of a preposition phrase). The Od is usually the direct object given and the Oi is usually the recipient. The following are examples of main or lexical verbs behaving as ditransitive verbs:

Mrs De Roza	gave	her new neighbours	some flowers.	OR
S	V	Oi	Od	
Mrs De Roza	gave	some flowers	to her new neighbours.	
S	V	Od	Oi	

The teacher	awarded	the best students	certificates.	OR
S	V	Oi	Od	
The teacher	awarded	certificates	to the best students.	
S	V	Od	Oi	

Tara	is baking	her friends	chocolate chip cookies.	OR
S	V	Oi	Od	
Tara	is baking	chocolate chip cookies	for her friends.	
S	V	Od	Oi	

Complex-Transitive Verbs (Verbs that Require Three Participants)

Complex-transitive verbs also require three participants. The participants are subject, object (by default the direct object here) and object complement. Typically, the clause pattern here will be S + V + O + Co. Complex-transitive verbs essentially equate the object to the object complement. The following are examples of main or lexical verbs behaving as complex-transitive verbs:

The film review committee	found	the new film	unsuitable for young audiences.
S	V	O	Co

The class	voted	Minh	the class president.
S	V	O	Co

We	named	our new puppy	Milo.
S	V	O	Co

It is important to note that verbs can behave differently in different contexts. For example, the verb 'make' can behave as a transitive, ditransitive or complex-transitive verb depending on the contexts in which it is used:

Kate	made (transitive)	some brownies
S	V	O

Kate	made (ditransitive)	Megan	some brownies.
S	V	Oi	Od

The brownies	made (complex-transitive)	Megan	very happy.
S	V	O	Co

There is one more very important clausal constituent that we need to discuss, and that is the adverbial. The adverbial is not a participant, but a circumstance. Circumstances are not required by the verb. These are optional constituents of the clause.

These functional constituents of subject, object, complement and adverbial may be expressed through various forms (note that the verb, as a functional constituent, may only be expressed through the form of a verb or verb phrase). The following are the different forms of phrases and clauses that these functional constituents can take. With reference to Chapter 5, it is important to take note that when functional constituents are clauses, there are implications for the types of sentences formed. For example, if the subject takes the form of a finite clause like *that he won the first prize* in a sentence like *That he won the first prize surprised everyone*, the sentence formed is that of a complex sentence as opposed to having a subject of a simple noun phrase form like *the results* in the simple sentence *The results surprised everyone*.

Subject

As English is a language with an SVO word order, the subject typically comes before the verb, and in a main clause, the subject must agree with the verb in number and person (commonly referred to as subject-verb agreement). For example, if the subject is singular and in the first person, as in, *I am the artist*, the verb to agree with the singular, first person subject *I* is *am* and not the plural *are*.

In Chapter 5, we said that main clauses (with the exception of the imperative sentence and ellipsis of shared subject in coordinated main clauses) must have a subject. The subject generally introduces what the clause is about, that is, the topic or theme of the clause. The subject can play a number of roles in a clause and this would depend on the verb being used. For example, in an active sentence with a transitive verb like *chased*, the subject is the animate agent or actor that initiates the action (verb). So, in an example like *Lee chased the dog*, *Lee* is the subject and the doer of the verb/action *chased*. Lee initiates the action *chased*. However, in an active sentence with a linking verb like *was* in for example, *Rosni was delighted*, the subject does not initiate the action, but rather experiences the feeling. As such, the subject is the experiencer here.

The different forms a subject can take are shown in Table 6.1.

Table 6.1 Forms of a subject.

Form	Function	Notes
noun phrase	The *little boy* plays at the playground daily. *He* likes the slides.	Pronouns are also noun phrases. Pronouns used as subjects will be subject pronouns like *he*, *she* and *they*.
preposition phase	*In the bag* is the book.	Some grammars refer to *in the bag* as an adverbial and *the book* as the subject as the singular verb *is* in fact agrees with the singular noun phrase *the book* (vs *In the bag are the books*, where the verb *are* agrees with the plural noun phrase *the books*.). Based on this analysis, there is 'locative inversion' where adverbials of location (in this case, *in the bag*) are inverted with the subject.

(*Continued*)

Table 6.1 (Continued)

Form	Function	Notes
finite clause	*That he won the first prize* surprised everyone. *Why she quit her job unexpectedly* is a mystery.	Finite clauses include *that*-clauses and *wh*-clauses. These clauses are considered grammatically singular.
non-finite *to*-infinitive clause	*To complete this project in three days* is impossible!	These clauses are considered grammatically singular.
non-finite participle clause	*Being kind to others* is my new year resolution.	These clauses are considered grammatically singular.

Object

In the English language, the object usually comes after the verb. For example, in the active sentence with the transitive verb *chased* in *Lee chased the dog*, *the dog* is the object. The object here plays the role of the patient or goal as it is affected by the action. Objects can play other roles depending on the verb being used. For example, in the active sentence *Ashraf drew a colourful rainbow*, *a colourful rainbow* is an object that does not play the role of a patient or goal, but rather a result (of the drawing).

It is important to note that only sentences with verbs that require objects can be passivised. The passive construction of *Lee chased the dog* is *The dog was chased by Lee* (note that in a passive sentence, the verb phrase takes the form of *be + -ed/en* participle). In the passive construction, the patient *the dog* thus becomes the subject.

Objects can be direct objects and indirect objects. As we discussed earlier, transitive verbs take a direct object, and ditransitive verbs take both a direct object and an indirect object. The direct object is the object directly affected by the action (verb), and the direct object may be animate or inanimate. The indirect object is usually the beneficiary or recipient of the direct object. Given that indirect objects are usually beneficiaries or recipients, they are either animate or personified (to make them human-like).

Let's first look at the different forms a direct object can take (verbs in the examples behave as transitive verbs), as shown in Table 6.2. Then we'll look at the different forms an indirect object can take (verbs in the examples behave as ditransitive verbs) in Table 6.3.

Table 6.2 Forms of a (direct) object.

Form	Function	Notes
noun phrase	James bakes *delicious muffins*. The children enjoy *them*.	Pronouns are also noun phrases. Pronouns used as objects will be object pronouns like *him, her* and *them*.

(*Continued*)

Table 6.2 (Continued)

Form	Function	Notes
preposition phrase	Reza asked *for a promotion*.	
finite clause	The teacher demanded *that the students submit their assignments the next day.* We know *what she did last summer.*	Finite clauses include *that*-clauses and *wh*-clauses.
non-finite *to*-infinitive clause	Rahman hopes *to meet his favourite soccer player.*	
non-finite participle clause	Zhixin likes *swimming in the ocean.*	

Table 6.3 Forms of an indirect object.

Form	Function	Notes
noun phrase	Hannah bought *her best friend* some chocolates. My mother sends *you* her best wishes.	Pronouns are also noun phrases. Pronouns used as objects will be object pronouns like *him*, *her* and *them*. The indirect object takes the form of a noun phrase when the indirect object comes directly after the verb.
preposition phrase	Hannah bought some chocolates *for her best friend*.	The indirect object takes the form of a preposition phrase when the indirect object comes after the direct object.

Complement

There are two types of complements – subject complements and object complements. A subject complement refers to the subject and expresses an attribute of the subject, while an object complement refers to the direct object and expresses an attribute of the direct object. This attribute may either characterise or identify the subject or the object in question (this distinction between characterising or identifying is elaborated below through examples).

Let's discuss subject complements first. Subjects complements occur with linking verbs like *be*, *become*, *seems* and *appear*. Earlier, we said that linking verbs essentially equate the subject to the subject complement. As such, a subject complement adds meaning to or completes the subject with an attribute as in the example, *Adam was happy*. In this example, *Adam* is the subject and *happy* is the subject complement that **characterises** Adam and completes the information about Adam. In another example, *Adam was the team leader*, Adam is the subject and *the team leader* is the subject complement that **identifies** Adam and completes the information about Adam.

The different forms a subject complement can take are shown in Table 6.4.

Table 6.4 Forms of a subject complement.

Form	Function	Notes
noun phrase	Ruanni is *a very caring teacher*.	
preposition phase	Those who lost their homes are *in misery*.	When preposition phrases that indicate positions or places after linking verbs, they are usually analysed as adverbials of place, and not subject complements. For example, in *Emily was in school*, the preposition phrase *in school* is an adverbial of place coming after the linking verb *is*, stating where Emily is. In this instance, *in school* is known as a compulsory adverbial as we cannot say **Emily is*. An adverbial of place that comes directly after a linking verb is compulsory, and an exception to the general rule that an adverbial is optional.
adjective phrase	Anna is *pretty in pink*.	
finite clause	The surprise is *that everyone agreed to the plan*. He is *what she has been looking for in a life partner*.	Finite clauses include *that*-clauses and *wh*-clauses.
non-finite *to*-infinitive clause	The school team seems *to be ready for the competition*.	

Object complements add meaning to or complete information about the direct objects in a clause and come directly after the object. Object complements occur with complex-transitive verbs. For example, in *Mai found her new classmate friendly*, where the verb *found* behaves as a complex-transitive verb, the object complement *friendly* characterises the object *her new classmate* and completes the information about *her new classmate*. It is her new classmate who is friendly. In another example, *Mai elected her new classmate the president of school council*, the object complement *the president of school council* identifies the object *her new classmate* and completes the information about her new classmate.

Table 6.5 presents the different forms an object complement can take (object is underlined for clarity).

Table 6.5 Forms of an object complement.

Form	Function	Notes
noun phrase	Angela considers <u>Amira</u> *her best friend*.	

(*Continued*)

Table 6.5 (Continued)

Form	Function	Notes
preposition phase	The class elected <u>Wai Kit</u> *as the class chairperson*.	
adjective phrase	The newspaper article made <u>her</u> *upset*.	
non-finite *-ing* clause	Mrs Ng discovered <u>her students</u> *cheating on the test*.	
non-finite *to*-infinitive clause	My grandfather encouraged <u>me</u> *to study hard*.	

Adverbial

As mentioned earlier, the adverbial is not a participant, but a circumstance. So, it is not a required constituent of the verb, and hence, the clause. Adverbials are optional constituents of the clause (except, as explained above, in the instance of compulsory adverbials). They answer, broadly, the questions of when, where, why and how of the verb. For example, in *Ken ate the cookie secretly in the bedroom*, there are two adverbials and these are *secretly* (answering the question of how of the verb *ate*) and *in the bedroom* (answering the question of where of the verb *ate*).

The different forms an adverbial can take are shown in Table 6.6.

Table 6.6 Forms of an adverbial.

Form	Function	Notes
noun phrase	*That June*, the twins turned one.	This example is an adverbial of time – answering the 'when' question of the verb *turned*.
preposition phase	The twins slept *in my bedroom*.	This example is an adverbial of place – answering the 'where' question of the verb *slept*.
adverb phrase	The twins are sleeping *soundly*.	This example is an adverbial of manner – answering the 'how' question of verb *visited*.
adjective phrase	*Excited to swim*, the twins ran to the pool.	The clause *to swim* modifies the adjective *excited* and this creates an adjective phrase. This example is an adverbial of reason – answering the 'why' question of verb *ran*. Note that there is another adverbial in the example, which is, the adverbial of place (answering the 'where' question) – *to the pool*.
finite clause	The twins attend art class *because they like drawing*.	This example is an adverbial of reason – answering the 'why' question of verb group *attend*.
non-finite clause	*While running in the park*, one of the twins fell.	This example is an adverbial of time – answering the 'when' question of verb *fell*.

Adverbials are the most flexible functional constituents in a clause as they are both optional and mobile, and there may be more than one adverbial in a clause. For example, in *Ken ate the cookie secretly in the bedroom*, the adverbials *secretly* and *in the bedroom* may both or individually be omitted and/or moved around in the clause. For example, we can say *Ken ate the cookie in the bedroom* (*secretly* is omitted) or *Secretly, Ken ate the cookie* (*in the bedroom* is omitted and *secretly* is moved upfront in position). Since an adverbial is not a required constituent of the verb, but an optional constituent answering the when, where, why and how questions of the verb, providing additional information to the clause, to include an adverbial in a clause is a grammatical choice of the writer. This choice will depend on the purpose, audience, context and culture of the text. This last point will be illustrated through the analyses of the following text excerpts.

Grammatical Functions as Meaning Making in Texts

The excerpts below are from *Where's Grandma* and have been analysed in terms of grammatical functions. The main verb phrase determining the structure of the clause/sentence has been bolded and the subject has been marked as S, the object as O, the subject complement as Cs, the object complement as Co and the adverbial as A. Additionally, time (when) adverbials are marked as A-T, place (where) adverbials as A-P, manner (how) adverbials as A-M (note that adverbials of manner analysed here are broad in meaning, capturing even, for example, adverbials of condition) and reason or purpose (why) adverbials as A-R.

EXCERPT 6.1

*When I was little (A-T), Grandma (S) **took** (V) me (O) to the nearby playground (A-P) every evening (A-T). She (S) **would hold** (V) my hand (O) as we walked through the void decks and car parks (A-M).*

*When we approached the playground (A-T), I (S) **would dash** to the swings (A-P) and then (A-T) [I (S) **would**] **feel** (V) Grandma's warm palms pushing my back (O) as I soared into the sky (A-M).*

EXCERPT 6.2

*Grandma (S) **would also** (A) **be** (V) around (A-P) to help (A-R) when I fell (A-T). She (S) **would check** (V) if I was alright (A-M) and [she (S) **would**] **encourage** (V) me (O) to get up on my feet (Co). If there was a wound (A-M), she (S) **would quickly** (A-M) **take** out (A-M) her handkerchief (O) to wipe away the blood (A-R).*

The analyses of the excerpts show that the verbs used are mainly transitive verbs and as such, the clauses in the text largely have an S-V-O structure, with a preponderance of adverbials. The subjects and objects of the clauses are mainly noun phrases, with several of the head nouns being pronouns. The choice to keep the structure of the subjects and objects simple as simple noun phrases is purposeful as the structures of the clauses become more complex with the numerous adverbials that largely take the form of subordinate clauses like *when I was little*, *as we walked through the void decks and car parks* and *if I was alright*. The addition of these subordinate clauses creates complex sentences (refer to Chapter 5 for a discussion of the types of sentences in this narrative) which then makes the narrative more complex in structure. Bearing in mind the target audience of this narrative, the author needs to balance the complexity of the structures used in the text. Having simple noun phrases as the subjects and objects help the young audience to follow through the text easily.

The numerous adverbials used in the excerpts play a critical role in advancing the purpose of this narrative, which is to share the story about Grandma who once used to be healthy and active, but then suffers the onset of Alzheimer's disease that is triggered by a fall. The use of adverbials of time help to toggle the narrative between the time when Grandma was healthy (for example, signalled by *when I was little*) and when Grandma was ill. Adverbials of place provide important details of where something occurred to help readers visualise the setting of the narrative, for example, readers can visualise Grandma taking Luke *to the playground*. Adverbials of manner also help readers visualise and even almost feel Grandma's care and concern for Luke, for example, the adverbial *if there was a wound* adds details of when Grandma would care for Luke. Adverbials of manner also add details of how certain actions took place in the narrative, once again, painting a visual picture of how the actions in the narrative took place, for example, in the use of the adverbial *as I soared into the sky*. Adverbials of reason used in narrative add supporting details of why an action was carried out, and in these excerpts, the adverbials of reason used like *to help* and *to wipe away the blood* construct Grandma as ever ready to help and care for Luke when she was healthy.

Let's look at an excerpt from another book, *Malaysian Flavours*, written by Malaysian writer Lee Su Kim. The book is a compilation of essays on the quirks and idiosyncrasies of Malaysians, where facets of Malaysian life are shared from the perspective of the author. The following excerpt from the essay 'At the Peranakan Dining Table' shares information on Peranakan dining practices and the excerpt is also almost instructive in nature as the author shares the dos and don'ts of Peranakan dining practices.

EXCERPT 6.3

> *The Peranakan culture is a unique blend of Malay and Chinese cultural elements <u>as a result of intermarriage between the Chinese and the local women in the days of the Malacca Sultanate five hundred years ago</u> (A-R).*
> <u>*When sitting down to a meal in an extended family setting*</u> *(A-T), age takes precedence <u>over gender</u> (A-M). <u>Thus</u> (A-M), older folks have the honour of taking their seats first followed by the young. It is considered rude <u>if</u>*

junior members of the family are seated before their elders (A-M). *In the old days* (A-T), it was unheard of to have the daughter-in-law already eating when the matriarch had not seated herself yet.

When all are seated (A-T), the younger ones are expected to 'call' their elders *before they tuck into the food* (A-T). This is *again* (A-M) a ritual to show respect for one's elders.

The excerpt has just been analysed for adverbials. Like the *Where's Grandma* excerpts, there are several different types of adverbials used. However, the role of the adverbials in this informative cum instructive text seems to differ from the adverbials used in the narrative. The adverbials of time, place, manner and reason used in the narrative advance the purpose of this narrative, which is to share the story about Grandma who once used to be healthy and active but now suffers from Alzheimer's disease. The adverbials in this excerpt from *Malaysian Flavours* do not advance any storyline, but rather by adding additional details, they serve to enrich the description of the cultural practices, anchoring them in time (for example, *in the old days*), providing context for the unique culture (for example, *as a result of intermarriage between the Chinese and the local women in the days of the Malacca Sultanate five hundred years ago*) and providing specifics of behaviours needed (being instructive) in the cultural practices (for example, *when all are seated* and *before they tuck into the food*). This allows the reader to better understand the practices being depicted.

Exploring Adverbials with 12-Year-Olds

In this section, we will examine HingMH's approach to introducing adverbials to her group of 12-year-old students. She teaches in a typical primary school located in the western region of the island, nestled within one of Singapore's suburban public housing estates. She is an experienced English teacher with an impressive teaching career spanning many years and has dedicated a considerable portion of her professional journey in this school. HingMH currently holds a senior position within the English department. HingMH's students required substantial guidance and support – they were low readiness learners, some of whom had special educational needs. She shared that they also had short attention spans and learnt differently which was why she had to often draw on the whiteboard to help them visualise more complex concepts.

HingMH explained that her current approach to teaching writing with the use of adverbials as a resource for meaning making is a stark contrast from her previous methods. In the past, she focused on asking Wh-questions to guide writing. Now, she emphasises the relationship between adverbials and verbs.

We look at how HingMH was successful at achieving her two objectives of helping her students understand the rationale behind using adverbials in writing and enabling them to effectively use adverbials to convey details related to time, place, manner and reason in sentences. To enable her students to understand what adverbials can do, HingMH used the metaphor of a rubber band – explaining to them that 'stretching a sentence' meant that it will 'tell us more about the verbs'.

For this lesson, HingHM chose to use an authentic Singaporean text – 'The Duck Thief'. It is a captivating short story set in 1940s Singapore, written by Chia Ah Hang. Part of the unpublished collection *Memories from the Kampung*, the story is narrated from the perspective of a young Ah Hang. The plot unfolds with growing excitement in the *kampung* (Malay: village) as the ducklings entrusted to Ah Hang's care mysteriously begin to disappear one by one.

HingHM and colleagues were introduced to the concept of mentor texts, also known as rich texts, in a previous project, so this was not their first experience with this approach. These authentic texts are carefully selected by the teacher to achieve several objectives: enhancing students' reading and writing skills, presenting complex content that encourages critical thinking, serving as exemplars that model effective grammar and text structure, and exposing learners to natural language usage to improve their ability to understand and produce language in real-life contexts.

HingMH started off with an engaging inductive approach where she read aloud two contrasting texts to her students. Text 1 was devoid of adverbials which she had deliberately removed from the original version. This resulted in a very concise and less captivating narrative. In contrast, the original Text 2 was embellished with adverbials, rendering it richer and more appealing.

Text 1 (Adapted)	Text 2 (Original) (HingMH's version was colour-coded) Adverbials of Place (A-P), Manner (A-M), Time (A-T), Reason (A-R)
Uncle Teck had a duck pond. Ah Hang sat down. His absolute favourite thing was to watch the ducks. Ah Hang liked the ducks.	*Uncle Teck **had** a duck pond <u>at the far end of the kampung</u>* (A-P). *Ah Hang **sat** <u>at the banks of the pond</u>* (A-P) *<u>after school</u>* (A-T) *<u>every day</u>* (A-T). *His absolute favourite thing was to watch the ducks. Ah Hang **liked** the ducks <u>because they swam back and forth</u>* (A-R). *He **liked** the ducks <u>because they waddled here and there</u>* (A-R). *He **liked** the ducks <u>because they never got wet</u>* (A-R).
Ah Hang noticed that one of the mother ducks had given birth to ducklings! 'One, two, three, four, five, six and SEVEN!' he counted. He ran and announced the good news.	*<u>One sunny afternoon</u>* (A-T), *Ah Hang **noticed** that one of the mother ducks had given birth to ducklings! 'One, two, three, four, five, six and SEVEN!' he **counted** <u>with glee</u>* (A-M). *He **ran** <u>quickly</u>* (A-M) *<u>to Uncle Teck</u>* (A-P) *and announced the good news.*

This glaring comparison immediately captured her students' attention and raised their curiosity. HingMH deliberately refrained from directly explaining the concept of adverbials but instead engaged her students in a discussion by asking them which text they preferred and why. This turned out to be an effective strategy instigating interest and creating an awareness of the significance of adverbials in writing.

HingMH then employed a pair work activity, allowing students to actively participate in comparing the two texts. She guided them in first pinpointing the verb followed by identifying and annotating adverbials, such as *had* (V) then *at the far end of the kampung* (A-P) or *liked* (V) then *because they never got wet* (A-R) which effectively denoted place and reason respectively. Students were encouraged to discuss and co-construct their understanding of how adverbials provided added details to verbs in a clause or sentence. This hands-on, exploratory phase equipped her students with a practical understanding of how adverbials function to enhance the content of their writing. HingMH shared at the interview that her students, after much probing, became clear that the writer was intentionally adding the information through adverbials. This led to a discussion about the possible intentions a writer might have to include adverbials. HingMH also shared that when her students had the chance to annotate themselves, they noticed that the 'additional information', that is, the adverbials, were answering the questions of when, where, why and how. This was indeed a breakthrough for her and her students.

Subsequently, HingMH explicitly taught the use of adverbials with the help of examples on slides. She explained how adverbials function and demonstrated how they can be employed to modify the verbs within clauses and sentences for greater clarity and depth. In a pair work activity, students were encouraged to stretch sentences using adverbials, providing them with an opportunity to actively apply their learning and further enhance their understanding.

HingMH's initial rationale for this series of lessons was to strengthen her students' writing skills by introducing the concept of adverbials. The effectiveness of her teaching can be seen in her approach to incorporate grammar teaching with listening, viewing, reading and writing skills. HingMH's teaching methods were quite remarkable. Her approach not only incorporated engagement, inductive reasoning, and practical application, it also created an environment in which students were supported in grasping and applying this grammar concept more effectively in their writing of narratives. HingMH said in the interview:

> When I was marking [their written pieces], I tried to write down *when, where, why, how* at the side of the piece to help me monitor what adverbials they were using and to show the students which were the ones that they usually used. For example, one piece had more *how* but not so many of the *when* and *why*. Of course, as writers, they do have a choice. So that's why I told them that if they felt that there isn't a need for extra information to add on to that particular sentence, that's fine. So in a way, I'm also showing them that I respect them as writers.
>
> (HingMH, Interview)

HingMH's approach not only empowered her students by actively involving them in their learning but also showcased her respect for them as writers who have their individual writing choices. By offering personalised feedback and encouraging autonomy, she created a supportive and engaging environment that significantly enhanced their understanding of adverbials as a meaning-making resource. This method not only improved their grasp of grammar but also instilled greater confidence in their abilities as writers.

In her interview and reflections, HingMH revealed that this experience was transformative for her as a language teacher. It marked the first time she had ventured into teaching adverbials without explicitly labelling them as such. She had to simplify her language and use metaphors, like stretching sentences 'like a rubber band,' to help her students grasp the concept. Her challenge was to convince her students that learning adverbials was worthwhile, emphasising that it did not require writing additional sentences but simply enhancing previously written sentences. The pair work activity, which boosted her students' confidence and allowed her to gain insights into their progress, was a valuable aspect of the experience. This collaborative approach not only made the learning process more engaging and less intimidating for HingMH's students but also provided a platform for immediate feedback and peer support. As a result, she found that her students were better able to apply their newfound knowledge in this supportive environment, fostering a deeper understanding and greater retention of how adverbials could be used in writing.

In all, HingMH found this teaching experience enriching, as it allowed her to refine her teaching approach and become more mindful of her students' needs. She focused on making language learning more meaningful and accessible, particularly for those who found it challenging.

Exploring Adverbials with 15-year-olds

Masyita, Nathan, Tasha and Norton worked collaboratively on this unit. Their school is a regular secondary school located in the eastern part of Singapore. The majority of their students live in the public housing estate which surrounds the school. The teachers shared that most of their students do not speak English at home. This lesson package was part of a larger unit, culminating in a final descriptive writing task, meant for their 15-year-olds. According to the teachers, they ranged from lower to middle-readiness. As a follow-up to a series of lessons on cohesion (between three to four weeks depending on the teacher/class) (note: these lessons on cohesion are elaborated on in Chapter 7), the teachers felt that it was necessary to extend the unit by designing an intervention focusing on the use of adverbials to improve their students' written descriptions. The planned writing task at the end of the unit was as follows:

> *Topic: Describe a person whom you admire and the ways in which his/her appearance and actions show his/her personality.*

You will be writing a descriptive essay of 350–500 words with a partner based on the above topic. Think of this task as creating linguistic snapshots/ videos of a person whom you look up to.
Consider the following questions:

1. *Who is this person you will be describing? How is he/she related to you?*
2. *What do you admire about this person? Is it his/her personality, certain traits he/she possesses and/or his/her physical appearance?*
3. *What does this person look like?*
4. *What does this person sound like?*
5. *Where do you usually interact with him/her?*
6. *What is this person's body language and gait (how he/she walks, steps or runs) usually like?*

Discuss the questions with your partner and jot down your responses below.
(Teaching artefact – handout)

Masyita, Nathan, Tasha and Norton opted to select an extract from Sunisa Manning's *A True Good Thai*. The choice was an interesting one. *A True Good Thai* explores the lives of Det, Chang and Lek against the backdrop of Thailand's political upheavals between 1973 and 1976. The protagonist Det, with royal lineage on his mother's side and a commoner father, grapples with societal expectations and political ideologies as he navigates military duty and relationships at Chulalongkorn University. Manning intricately weaves historical events and personal dilemmas to highlight the complexities of Thai identity and activism during a tumultuous period in the country's history. Notably, the novel and extract chosen are rich in descriptions, making them ideal for teaching cohesion and adverbials, as they offer ample opportunities for exploring how the focused grammar is used to maintain the flow of the narrative and to create vivid descriptions.

The students had already written a first draft applying what they had learnt about cohesive devices. However, the teachers felt that the drafts fell short of expectations. Tasha shared that their students often struggled to produce substantial content especially in descriptive pieces. Many students did not know what to focus on and encountered difficulty writing beyond simple descriptions. Noticing that the written pieces by the students lacked descriptive elements, the teachers decided to focus again on the use of adverbials. Masyita explained:

> As we were teaching descriptive writing, it was important that the students were able to describe the subject matter in a vivid manner. Hence, the use of adverbials was essential in helping them extend their ideas.
> (Masyita's reflection)

The teachers planned an extensive intervention to revisiting the use of adverbials and how they could be used more effectively in descriptive writing. The activities were extensive – some of which included the viewing and discussion of a Thai commercial, close reading of authentic excerpts from the chosen text, whole class explicit teaching, group/pair discussion and scaffolded writing activities. This section, however, will highlight two grammar as meaning-making activities that helped their students with their descriptive writing.

In one of the activities, students were introduced to an excerpt from *A Good True Thai*. The teachers went through a close reading of the excerpt with adverbials annotated. The teachers also tried to elicit the importance of adverbials and their purpose in descriptive writing. The de-construction of this excerpt was done 'sentence by sentence' according to Nathan. He also admitted that 'initially [there] was very much handholding'. The following is the annotated excerpt used (the abbreviations used – A-P, A-M and A-T – stand for adverbials of place, manner and time, respectively).

EXCERPT 6.4

Just ahead is a crowd of girls. One tall girl shrieks <u>as she rolls a peeled longan in her outstretched hands</u> (A-T or A-M). Thick strands of black hair cascade <u>down her back</u> (A-M or A-P) and flow <u>over her shoulders</u> (A-M or A-P), <u>reaching her ribcage</u> (A-P). 'Don't make me eat it!' she cries.

Look at her hands, slim and tapered. That upward turn at their tips, perfect for Thai dancing. Det watches the seniors push the 'eyeball' towards her. She chews it <u>at the front of her mouth</u> (A-P), lips pursed <u>until she recognises the taste</u> (A-T).

<u>Laughing</u> (A-M), the seniors pull the blindfold <u>from her face</u> (A-P). Det starts. She's Chinese. He can tell <u>by the way they flock around her</u> (A-M) that they find her attractive too. She's brushing her hair <u>out of her face</u> (A-M), and turns her attention <u>from person to person</u> (A-M) <u>as she congratulates them on the trick</u> (A-T). Their eyes meet; Det flicks his gaze <u>up the beach</u> (A-P).

He climbs a low dune, brushes sand <u>off a different log</u> (A-P), straightens the crease of his pants. <u>As he turns to sit</u> (A-T), the girl appears. She presses her perfect hands <u>together</u> (A-M) <u>in a greeting</u> (A-M) and seats herself, <u>tilting back with a sigh</u> (A-M). The wind whips her hair <u>into a small hurricane</u> (A-M). She lets it fly, <u>closing her eyes</u> (A-M). Everything about her is long: long hair, long face that ends in a pointed chin, long limbs that seem to go on forever.

'What did they make you do?' she asks. Her eyes are deep black half-moons <u>in a startlingly pale face</u> (A-P). <u>Though she speaks seriously</u> (A-M), her cheeks create triangles that frame and lead his eyes <u>to the peaked indent of her full top lip</u> (A-P).

(Annotated excerpt from *A True Good Thai*)

This strategy of close reading with annotated adverbials provided teachers with a valuable tool for awareness raising of grammar and reading and writing development. By breaking down the text 'sentence by sentence,' teachers effectively demonstrated how adverbials contributed to descriptive writing in the authentic piece, enhancing students' understanding of adverbial usage within context. Furthermore, this approach allowed the teachers to illustrate the purpose and impact of adverbials on the overall quality of writing and empowered their students to apply these techniques in their own writing to create more vivid and engaging descriptive pieces. It is worth noting that the adverbials in this excerpt are directly related to the characters, which aligns with the skills needed for the final writing task.

Employing a similar strategy to HingMH, the teachers got their students to compare two excerpts from the text – the original with rich adverbials and an adapted one stripped of all its adverbials:

Adapted	Original
The seniors pull the blindfold. Det starts. She's Chinese. He can tell that they find her attractive too. She's brushing her hair and turns her attention. Their eyes meet; Det flicks his gaze.	*<u>Laughing</u>, the seniors pull the blindfold <u>from her face</u>. Det starts. She's Chinese. He can tell <u>by the way they flock around her</u> that they find her attractive too. She's brushing her hair <u>out of her face</u> and turns her attention <u>from person to person</u> <u>as she congratulates them on the trick</u>. Their eyes meet; Det flicks his gaze <u>up the beach</u>.*

The teachers were generally pleased that the lessons turned out well. As Masyita shared, her students used to see grammar as only useful for editing exercises but now they see grammar as more than that. She also said that her students appeared to enjoy the lessons: 'Compared to their earlier pieces of writing, I could see that there was more effort in lengthening their ideas and sentences using adverbials in the final draft of their descriptive essay' (Masyita's reflection).

Nathan, in his interview, summed it up very nicely when he shared that 'adverbials are tools for our students to stretch their writing . . . when they learn to focus on the details which adverbials allows them to do, they're giving us added understanding of what is happening'. He also shared that most of his students were able to do it – some with a higher degree of success than others.

In witnessing what HingMH, Masyita, Nathan, Tasha and Norton have done with adverbials and the authentic texts which accompanied their lessons, it is evident that there is a collective belief among them that adverbials are integral to the meaning-making process in reading and writing. HingMH's engaging inductive methods illustrate how adverbials, when incorporated into writing, stretch sentences to convey richer details about verbs, emphasising the significance of grammar in enhancing the substance of narratives and other types of writing. Similarly, Masyita, Nathan, Tasha and Norton intentionally integrated adverbials into their lessons on descriptive writing, recognising that adverbials play a crucial role in extending ideas and creating vivid linguistic snapshots. In both schools, there was a clear a shift from traditional grammar instruction to a dynamic understanding of grammar as a tool for effective communication, demonstrating how these educators skilfully intertwined grammatical concepts with practical applications, fostering a deeper understanding of language as a vehicle for meaningful expression.

Extracts used in Chapter 6

The following is the extract from 'At the Peranakan Dining Table', from *Malaysian Flavours*, written by Lee Su Kim.

The Peranakan culture is a unique blend of Malay and Chinese cultural elements as a result of intermarriage between the Chinese and the local women in the days of the Malacca Sultanate five hundred years ago.

When sitting down to a meal in an extended family setting, age takes precedence over gender. Thus, older folks have the honour of taking their seats first followed by the young. It is considered rude if junior members of the family are seated before their elders. In the old days, it was unheard of to have the daughter-in-law already eating when the matriarch had not seated herself yet.

When all are seated, the younger ones are expected to 'call' their elders before they tuck into the food. This is again a ritual to show respect for one's elders. It would go something like this, in order of seniority: Kong, makan (Grandpa, eat); Po, makan (Grandma, eat); Nya, makan (Mother, eat); Toa Chi, makan (Big Sister, eat); Ko, makan (Big Brother, eat); and so on. The elders can respond with a brief reply makan, nod slightly or ignore the addressee altogether.

The following is the extract from 'The Duck Thief', from *Memories of the Kampung*, written by Chia Ah Hang.

Uncle Teck had a duck pond at the far end of the kampung. Ah Hang's pastime was to sit at the banks of the pond after school every day. His absolute favourite thing was to watch the ducks.

Ah Hang liked that the ducks because swam back and forth. He liked that the ducks because they waddled here and there. He liked the ducks because they never got wet.

One sunny afternoon, Ah Hang noticed that one of the mother ducks had given birth to ducklings! 'One, two, three, four, five, six and SEVEN!' he counted with glee. He ran quickly to Uncle Teck and announced the good news.

'Very good Ah Hang,' Uncle Teck beamed happily, 'I would like you to look after them for me now.' Uncle Teck told him that for a couple of years now, ducklings at the pond have been disappearing mysteriously. Ah Hang was over the moon! He had a real responsibility!

This was to become Ah Hang's new preoccupation from that day on. Whenever he arrived at the pond, he would count, "one, two, three, four, five, six, seven." And to be very sure, he would carefully count again several minutes later.

For a week, Ah Hang kept this up. He would count the ducklings five times until his mother called him back home for dinner.

Then on the eighth day, something very strange happened.

'One, two, three, four, five, six . . . one, two, three, four, five, six . . .'

Twice Ah Hang counted but there were only six? Only six ducklings!

He started getting worried as he counted for a third time, 'One, two, three, four, five, s . . .'

Before his very eyes, the sixth duckling disappeared suddenly! It seemed to be sucked below the surface of the pond!

'Uncle Teck! Uncle Teck!' Ah Hang yelled frantically while keeping his eyes glued on the remaining five. 'Someone's stealing our ducklings! Please come! NOW!' By this time, his eyes were brimmed with tears because he had grown so attached to his feathered friends.

The following is the extract from A True Good Thai (pp. 33–34), written by Sunisa Manning.

Just ahead is a crowd of girls. One tall girl shrieks as she rolls a peeled longan in her outstretched hands. Thick strands of black hair cascade down her back and flow over her shoulders, reaching her rib cage. 'Don't make me eat it!' she cries.

Look at her hands, slim and tapered. The upward turn at their tips perfect for Thai dancing. Det watches the seniors push the 'eyeball' towards her. She chews it at the front of her mouth, lips pursed until she recognises the taste.

Laughing, the seniors pull the blindfold from her face. Det starts. She's Chinese. He can tell by the way they flock around her that they find her attractive too. She's brushing her hair out of her face, and turns her attention from person to person as she congratulates them on the trick. The ice meet; Det flicks his gaze up the beach.

He climbs a low dune, brushes sand off a different log, straightens the crease of his pants. As he turns to sit, the girl appears. She presses her perfect hands together in a greeting and seats herself, tilting back with a sigh. The wind whips her hair into a small hurricane. She lets it fly, closing her eyes. Everything about her is long: long hair, long face that ends in a pointed chin, long limbs that seem to go on forever.

'What did they make you do?' she asks. Her eyes are deep black half-moons in a startling pale face. Though she speaks seriously, her cheeks create triangles that frame and lead his eyes to the peaked indent of her full top lip.

'Me?'

'I'm Lek,' she says, dipping her head. She speaks in flawless Thai with no twists of a Chinese accent. And she looks – she has the look of the lantom

three, the way it stands in the wind, sways and is not broken. The arched branches, the oblong leaves, the spray of milky flowers with a deep gold drop.

'I'm Det.' He manages to sound unsure of his name. He clears his throat, wondering if he should have snapped open his full name and title like an umbrella giving shade. Mom Luang Akarand, pleased to meet you, but call me Det.

References

Chia, A.H. (2020). The duck thief. In *Memories of the Kampung*. Unpublished.
Lee, S.K. (1997). *Malaysian Flavours*. MPH Publishing.
Manning, S. (2020). *A True Good Thai*. Epigram Books.

7 Cohesion and Coherence

What Is Cohesion?

Cohesion refers to the way words, phrases, clauses, sentences and paragraphs are linked to create texts which are clear, organised and smooth in flow. According to Halliday and Hasan (1995), influential linguists in the study of cohesion, cohesion refers to

> **relations of meaning** that exist within the text, and that define it as a text. Cohesion occurs where **the interpretation of some element** in the discourse is dependent on that of another. The one **presupposes the other**, in the sense that it cannot be effectively decoded except by recourse to it. When this happens, **a relation of cohesion is set up** and the two elements, the presupposing and the presupposed, are thereby at least potentially integrated into a text.
> (Halliday & Hasan, 1995, p. 4; emphasis added)

This definition captures the essence of cohesion which is the interconnectedness established within a text. For there to be cohesion within a text, relations between lexical and grammatical items are intentionally and explicitly created between and across words, phrases, clauses, sentences and paragraphs. When there are relations set up this way, a text is recognised as a unified whole, rather than a set of unconnected or unrelated words, phrases, clauses and sentences.

Cohesion is realised through **cohesive devices** which are linguistic elements used to create links and connections across different levels - words, phrases, clauses, sentences and paragraphs. According to Halliday and Matthiessen (2004), cohesion is established through lexicogrammatical resources - both lexical links which are lexical cohesive devices that create lexical cohesion, and grammatical links which are grammatical cohesive devices that create grammatical cohesion.

DOI: 10.4324/9781003255963-7

Lexical Cohesive Devices

Lexical links across lexical items – words, phrases, clauses, sentences and paragraphs – can be achieved through, for example,

- Repetition of words or phrases.
- Use of words or phrases that are related in meaning. For example:
    - synonyms (or near-synonyms)
    - antonyms
    - hyponyms
    - meronyms
    - lexical sets
- Structurally related words (words that share the same root or stem word).

The various lexical cohesive devices that create relations between lexical elements will be explained and illustrated through the analysis of an excerpt from *Take-Off*, a narrative written by writer, Dennis Yeo (extract of narrative is found at the end of the chapter). *Take-Off* is a narrative about a young Singaporean man who is leaving Singapore to pursue his studies in the United States. It captures the thoughts and emotions of the young man as he says goodbye to his parents and girlfriend. The narrative is set in Changi Airport as he gets ready to board his flight.

EXCERPT 7.1

> *The future was so sure and yet so uncertain. Things happened so quickly after that. Enrolling online, arranging accommodation, securing bank loans, shopping for winter clothes, having farewell dinner after farewell supper and stuffing every possession and memory one could carry into a suitcase that was now on a conveyor belt heading towards the cargo hold of the belly of an aircraft. Leaving home was both difficult and exciting. He felt like a ship that had cast off its moorings, sailing off towards a destination that lay beyond the horizon, knowing it was there but not actually seeing it.*
>
> *He stopped at a huge globe that dominated the entrance of Planet Traveler. He would be further than he had ever been from home, almost a third of the circumference of the Earth. A couple kissing in a corner caught him stealing a glance in their direction. He liked how airports normalised all public displays of affection. Anyone watching would just assume that this would be the last time in a long time they would see each other so any physical contact was not just nudgingly accepted, but quietly envied. He thought of her. How would this affect them? He had heard how difficult it was to maintain a long-distance relationship. Three years apart, maybe four. Yes, he would return, but things would be different.*

They both knew that this would tear them apart, but none dared to say it to the other, preferring instead to say what the other wanted to hear. Sweet nothings of how they would WhatsApp every day, how she would fly over and visit, how much they would miss each other, how what they felt would not change. Whoever said that absence made the heart grow fonder was a liar. Somehow, the physical body has to be present for someone to be fully and always remembered. She would meet some hunk at NUS and he would be there for her while he was 'virtually there'. Maybe he would meet someone too, a hot ang mo girl perhaps. The only constant, besides change, was that life would move on.

(Note: *ang mo* originates from Hokkien and is used, largely in Singapore and Malaysia, to refer to a white person.)

Repetition of Words and Phrases

When words or phrases are repeated within and across sentences and paragraphs in a text, there is a sense of continuity and unity established within the text. The repeated words or phrases show how ideas across the text are related. Such repetition also emphasises the main ideas or themes of the text and draws readers' attention to these central ideas and themes. When words or phrases are repeated, there is also clarity of the main ideas in the text, allowing the readers to easily follow the flow of the text, aiding comprehension of the text.

In this excerpt, there are several words that have been repeated. Some examples of these words are *farewell, home, apart* and *change*. The repetition of these words in this excerpt is significant as these are the core ideas or themes of the text. This text is about saying farewell as the protagonist is leaving his home, Singapore, saying goodbye to his parents and his girlfriend. He will be apart from his loved ones and will experience changes in this process, possibly including changes in his relationship with his girlfriend.

Synonyms

Synonyms are words with very closely related meanings. The use of synonyms is a way of reducing repetition and introducing variation to a text, while maintaining the semantic links within the text. There is still focus on the same ideas and hence continuity of these ideas. The use of synonyms also allows for more clarity of the text as the use of different words with similar meanings would allow readers to clarify the meaning of how these words are used in the text.

In this excerpt, there are words that are similar in meaning. For example, *supper* and *dinner* in *farewell supper* and *farewell dinner* are near synonyms and in using these near synonyms, with the repeated word *farewell*, the author is emphasising the number of farewell gatherings that took place because of the protagonist's departure.

Another pair of near synonyms used in the excerpt, one might argue, is *hunk* and *hot ang mo girl*. These are near synonyms referring to potential attractive male and female partners that the protagonist and his girlfriend may respectively find since they will be apart. One may argue that this points to the theme of change in the text.

Antonyms

Antonyms are words with opposite or contrastive meanings. The use of words with opposite meaning across a text allows for relationships and links to be established within the text, contributing to the continuity and unity of the text. Like the use of synonyms within a text, the use of antonyms allows for semantic links to be established in a text.

In the following sentences from the excerpt, two pairs of possible antonyms, *sure* and *uncertain* and *difficult* and *exciting* are identified:

> *The future was so <u>sure</u> and yet so <u>uncertain</u>.*
> *Leaving home was both <u>difficult</u> and <u>exciting</u>.*

The use of these antonyms shows the conflict of emotions the protagonist is going through as he embarks on this new journey, leaving home and his loved ones behind. The use of these antonyms strengthens the running theme of change in the text.

Hyponyms

A type-of or member-of relationship between a general word and a specific word sets up a relationship of hyponymy. Hyponymy is a hierarchical relationship where the meaning of the specific word is included in the meaning of the general word. The general word or term is known as the superordinate or the hypernym and the specific words or instances are known as hyponyms. The hierarchical relationship creates relations between a hypernym and its hyponyms, thus structuring and organising the relationship between words in a text (that is, information) for better understanding. This hierarchical relationship also allows for elaboration of the hypernym, which can be a topic, idea, concept or item, by providing details of the hypernym through the use of hyponyms as instances of the hypernym. Hyponymy thus allows for links to be made between specific and general topics, ideas, concepts or items within a text, structuring and organising a piece of text, and once again contributing to the continuity and unity of the text. The text is then more accessible to the readers.

One could argue that a relationship of hyponymy is set up between *all public displays of affection* (hypernym) and *kissing* (hyponym) in these sentences from the excerpt:

A couple <u>kissing</u> in a corner caught him stealing a glance in their direction. He liked how airports normalised <u>all public displays of affection</u>.

In the context of this airport scene, *kissing* is a type of *public display of affection*. The use of hyponymy here contextualises the specific behaviour of *kissing* within the general idea of *all public displays of affection* in the context of the narrative, that is, the airport. This contributes to the overall cohesion of the text.

Meronyms

Meronymy is yet another hierarchical relationship. Meronymy is a part-of relationship between a general or a superordinate word, called a holonym, and a specific word, called a meronym. A relationship between the whole (which can be a topic, idea, concept or item) and its parts (or components) is created within a text when meronymy is used. Through the use of meronymy, information about a particular subject matter (the whole) is then organised in relation to its components (the parts). Such an organisation of information within a text links different parts of the text, creating unity in the text. Meronymy also aids the comprehension of a text by the reader as it allows for a whole to be discussed in terms of its parts, breaking down, perhaps, a more complex topic, idea, concept or item, into its smaller parts.

In this excerpt, there are several examples of meronymy:

Enrolling online, arranging accommodation, securing bank loans, shopping for winter clothes, having farewell dinner after farewell supper and stuffing every possession and memory one could carry into a suitcase that was now on a <u>conveyor belt</u> heading towards the <u>cargo hold</u> of the belly of an <u>aircraft</u>.

In the above section of the excerpt, *cargo hold* (meronym) is part of an *aircraft* (holonym). *Conveyor belt* and *aircraft* may also be analysed as parts of the larger entity, the airport, which is the context of this narrative.

Through the use of meronymy, relationships are set up between wholes and parts, creating links and unity in the text.

Another example of meronymy is in the following:

Whoever said that absence made the <u>heart</u> grow fonder was a liar. Somehow, the <u>physical body</u> has to be present for someone to be fully and always remembered.

The whole is the *physical body* and the part of is the *heart*. The use of meronymy here in this excerpt emphasises that the presence of the whole (*physical body*) is more important than just the part (*heart*). This instance of meronymy foregrounds another theme of the narrative, which is, being apart, thereby creating continuity in the text.

Lexical Sets

A lexical set comprises words or phrases from the same lexical field or words or phrases related to a particular topic. When words or phrases from the same field or topic are used, there are semantic connections and links between these words and phrases, tightening the focus on the main idea, topic or theme of a text. In this way, there is a common thread running through the text, making the text a unified whole. Readers are also better able to follow or comprehend a piece of text if words or phrases related to the same idea, topic or theme run through the text.

In the excerpt, the following lexical set contributes to building up the setting of the narrative, which is the airport – *conveyor belt, cargo hold, aircraft, Planet Traveller,* and *globe*. With the use of words or phrases related to the lexical set of 'airport' spread throughout the narrative, the reader is constantly reminded that the setting is in an airport and is almost able to visualise this setting. This establishes cohesion in the text.

Another example of a lexical set in the excerpt is one that focuses on one of the main themes of the narrative, 'being apart' – *long distance, absence, 'virtually there', fly over and visit* and *miss each other*. The use of these words or phrases belonging to the same theme of 'being apart' runs through the text, building on nuances of this theme, making the text a unified whole.

Structurally Related Words

The use of structurally related words that share a common root word within a text also creates relations between words in a text, thus contributing to the unity of the text. When structurally related words are used within a text, there is morphological consistency within the text that will facilitate the comprehension of the text. This is because these morphologically related words which are built from the same root word are similar-looking words which share similar meanings. The text is then more accessible to readers as the words used in the text are related. The use of structurally related words within a text also means the ideas these words refer to are repeated in the text, and so in this way, the ideas are emphasised, maintaining a focus on these ideas. This will help readers once again follow the flow of the text better.

In this excerpt, there are no examples of structurally related words that share a common root word (note: for a text to be cohesive, there is no need for the presence of all cohesive devices). To illustrate how structurally related words can create lexical cohesion, let's look at the following example:

> *The beautifully crafted wooden table was made by an experienced carpenter. The beautiful table won the first prize at the international craftmanship competition.*

There are two pairs of words which are structurally related here, sharing the same root words. These are *beautifully* and *beautiful* (same root word 'beautiful') and, *crafted* and *craftmanship* (same root word 'craft'). Given that these pairs of words are related in form and in meaning, there is continuity and hence cohesion, emphasising that the table was visually appealing and well-made.

Grammatical Cohesive Devices

Links within a text are not only made using lexical cohesive devices. Grammatical links across words, phrases, clauses, sentences and paragraphs can also be achieved through grammatical cohesive devices such as the following:

- reference
- ellipsis
- substitution
- conjunction
- repetition of structures

The various grammatical cohesive devices will be explained and illustrated through the analysis of another excerpt from *Take-Off*.

EXCERPT 7.2

> *He scrolled through his history on his Facebook wall. It was a time capsule that chronicled his thoughts, emotions, relationships, interests, life events, chats, pictures, wisecracks. It was a junkyard of his nonsense, impulsively uploaded and conveniently timelined. It was his life in words and pictures shared with his 509 friends, 487 of whom would not even realise he was gone. He wondered how things would be different between him and his friends. He smiled as he came across a post or an Instagram of an event that he remembered fondly. Many people dissed social media but to him this was life in 2D and his lifeline to the people who really meant something to him, no matter how tenuous those bonds were.*
>
> *He typed 'I am outta here. See you on the other side.', hit the Enter button, logged out and joined the queue at the boarding gate. He was travelling light, just a haversack with his laptop in it, and a winter jacket, in case it was cold when he arrived. Past the metal detector and the X-ray checkpoints, he handed his documents to a lady in the signature sarong kebaya. Smile.*

Boarding pass check. Name check. Passport check. Name check. Face check. Welcome aboard. Smile. Next.

The departure gate was filling up. It was a full flight, long haul. His fellow pilgrims included solo travelers taking a quick snooze or reading or making final changes on their laptops before boarding. He remembered his first flight on his own without his family on a China Airlines flight bound for Taiwan for an in-camp training during his National Service. Around him were also couples inextricably entwined stealing pecks oblivious to anyone around them, and families with father and mother confirming if they had switched off the hall lights as their children looked out the glass at the humongous bird. He had to SMS his Dad. His Dad did not use a smartphone.

Reference

Reference refers to the grammatical resources that a speaker or writer can use to indicate whether a certain someone or something has been mentioned before in a text (for example, through the use of pronouns), and so is now repeated or whether this someone or something is a new mention (for example, through the use of articles). In this way, reference has got to do with identifiability (Halliday and Matthiessen, 2004). It is important to note that this repetition or new mention is in relation to what was mentioned or not in the text, and not with reference to the context. When reference points to someone or something in a text, this is known as endophoric reference. When reference points to someone or something outside of a text, this is known as exophoric reference. We are only concerned with endophoric reference, and not exophoric reference, as when we talk about cohesive devices, we are talking about devices that make links within a text (co-text) and not between the text and the outside (context).

When we use reference to point backwards to someone or something that was explicitly mentioned earlier in a text, this is known as anaphoric reference. On the other hand, when we use reference to point forward to someone or something that is explicitly mentioned later in a text, this is known as cataphoric reference. Anaphoric reference is much more common than cataphoric reference.

There are three main types of cohesive reference, according to Halliday and Matthiessen (2004). They are personal reference, demonstrative reference and comparative reference. The following is an elaboration on these types of cohesive reference.

Personal Reference

Personal reference has to do with the category of the person. Included in this category are singular and plural personal pronouns and singular and plural possessive determiners. Examples of singular personal pronouns are *he, she, him*, *her* and *it*, and the plural personal pronouns are *they* and *them*. These personal pronouns stand in for a noun phrase and can stand on their own. Examples of singular possessive determiners are *his*, *her* and *its*. The plural possessive determiner is *their*. Possessive determiners always come together with nouns and they do not stand on their own.

In the excerpt, the third-person personal masculine pronoun *he* and *him* is repeatedly used to refer to the protagonist. What is interesting in this narrative is that there is no explicit mention of the protagonist. The name of the protagonist is never mentioned. As such, the repeated use of *he* and *him* maintains the cohesive links across the text. There are other instances of the use of personal reference in the excerpt. Let's look at the following section from the excerpt above:

> *He scrolled through his history on <u>his Facebook wall</u>. <u>It</u> was a time capsule that chronicled his thoughts, emotions, relationships, interests, life events, chats, pictures, wisecracks. <u>It</u> was a junkyard of his nonsense, impulsively uploaded and conveniently timelined. <u>It</u> was his life in words and pictures shared with his 509 friends, 487 of whom would not even realise he was gone.*

The repeated use of the third-person personal neutral pronoun *it* is used as anaphoric reference to refer back to the first mention of *his Facebook wall*. The repeated use of *it* creates a reference chain and ties this section of the excerpt together, as all instances of *it* refers to *his Facebook wall*.

As for the use of possessive determiners as reference in the excerpt, the possessive determiner *his* is used repeatedly to refer back to the protagonist who is referred to by the pronoun *he*. This creates links across the excerpt, creating cohesion. Here is an example where the possessive determiner *his* in *his laptop* refers back to *he* who is the protagonist:

> <u>*He*</u> *was travelling light, just a haversack with <u>his</u> laptop in it, and a winter jacket, in case it was cold when he arrived.*

Here is another sentence from the excerpt:

> *Around him were also couples inextricably entwined stealing pecks oblivious to anyone around them, and families with <u>father and mother</u> confirming if they had switched off the hall lights as <u>their</u> children looked out the glass at the humongous bird.*

The possessive determiner *their* in *their children* refers back to *father and mother*. Once again, links are created in the excerpt with the use of determiners.

Demonstrative Reference

Demonstrative reference has to do with proximity from the point of view of the speaker or writer. Examples of demonstratives are the 'near' specific pronouns like *this* and *these*, the 'far', specific pronouns like *that* and *those* and the non-specific pronoun *it*. Other demonstratives are the 'near' specific determiners like *this* and *these* and the 'far', specific determiners like *that* and *those*. The 'near' adverb *here* and the 'far' adverb *there* are also included as demonstratives.

Here is a sentence from the excerpt where the demonstrative pronoun *this* is used as anaphoric reference to create cohesion by referring back to *social media*:

> Many people dissed <u>social media</u> but to him <u>this</u> was life in 2D and his lifeline to the people who really meant something to him, no matter how tenuous those bonds were.

The demonstrative 'near' pronoun *this* is used because the referent *social media* is 'near' from the writer's point of view, almost immediately mentioned before.

The definite article *the* is also included as a demonstrative. However, *the* does not refer to proximity in relation to the speaker or writer's point of view. The demonstrative *the* just signals whether the identity of the noun it comes with is specific or not, that is, whether it had been previously mentioned or is known by both the speaker/writer and listener/reader.

Let's look at another sentence in the excerpt:

> Past <u>the</u> metal detector and <u>the</u> X-ray checkpoints, he handed his documents to <u>a</u> lady in the signature sarong kebaya.

The indefinite article *a* or *an* is usually used when there is first mention of someone or something in a text. In the example sentence above, the indefinite article *a* in *a lady in the signature sarong kebaya* signals that a new character is being introduced in the narrative. Why then is the definite article *the* used in *the metal detector* and *the X-ray checkpoints* when these are also first mentions in the narrative? This is because the definite article *the* is also used to signal the known when there is shared knowledge and experience between the writer and the reader – in this case, the setting of the narrative is in an airport and it is shared knowledge that in an airport, there are metal detectors and X-ray checkpoints as part of security measures. This shared knowledge can be attributed to the expected lexical set associated with an airport – in which metal detectors and X-ray checkpoints are expected items.

Comparative Reference

As seen from the illustrations of personal reference and demonstrative reference, these two types of references set up relationships of co-reference where the same entity is referred to again. Comparative reference, on the other hand, is a type of cohesive reference that involves making comparisons. When comparisons are involved, an entity or concept is compared to a previously mentioned entity or concept in the text. In this way, there is reference back to an entity or concept being mentioned earlier, thereby creating cohesion in a text. To compare, one may use comparative adjectives like *same, different, identical, prettier* and *heavier*, or comparative adverbs like *more, less, better* and *similarly*. Ordinal numbers like *second* and *fifth* may also be used to compare.

Let's look at an instance of comparative reference used as a cohesive device in the excerpt:

> He remembered his <u>first</u> flight on his own without his family on a China Airlines flight bound for Taiwan for an in-camp training during his National Service.

In this sentence, the ordinal *first* used in *his first flight on his own without his family on a China Airlines flight bound for Taiwan for an in-camp training during his National Service* signals that this flight he is taking to San Francisco is not his first solo flight. In this way, the comparison contributes to contextualising the narrative, giving readers more insight into the protagonist's experiences, perhaps situating him as an experienced solo traveller. The use of comparative reference then contributes to the cohesion of the text.

Ellipsis

With ellipsis, parts of a structure (in the contexts of the noun phrase, verb phrase or the clause) may be left out in a text and the reader or listener will have to retrieve this 'missing' element from elsewhere in the text. In this way, links are created within the text.

In the excerpt, there are several instances of ellipsis, prompting readers to look within the text to retrieve the missing information. When ellipsis prompts readers to do this, links are established within the text.

Let's look at the following section of the excerpt:

> He scrolled through his history on <u>his Facebook wall</u>. It was a time capsule that chronicled his thoughts, emotions, relationships, interests, life events, chats, pictures, wisecracks. It was a junkyard of his nonsense, impulsively uploaded and conveniently timelined. It was his life in words and pictures shared with his 509 friends, 487 of whom would not even realise he was gone. He wondered how things would be different between him and his friends. He smiled as he came across a post or an Instagram of an event that he remembered fondly. Many people dissed social media but to him this was life in 2D and his lifeline to the people who really meant something to him, no matter how tenuous those bonds were.
>
> He typed 'I am outta here. See you on the other side', <u>hit the Enter button, logged out and joined the queue at the boarding gate</u>.

There is ellipsis in the last sentence of this section of the excerpt and the retrieved information is included in the brackets:

He typed 'I am outta here. See you on the other side', (he) <u>hit the Enter button (of his Facebook wall), (he) logged out (of his Facebook wall) and (he) joined the queue at the boarding gate</u>.

It is common to omit the repeated mention of the same subject in coordinated clauses as done so in the above analysis – the subject *he* is omitted in the coordinated clauses as this can be easily retrieved from the first mention of the subject in the sentence. The ellipsis of the subject not only links the clauses with the retrieval of this information, but also avoids the repeated mention of the subject *he*, creating a smoother flow of the sentence.

The other instances of ellipsis are of the repeated phrase of his Facebook wall. Readers will have to retrieve this missing information – hit the Enter button of what?, logged out of what? – from the paragraph before which mentions that the protagonist was on his Facebook wall. In this way, links are then established across the text, establishing cohesion.

Another example of an instance of ellipsis is in the following section of the excerpt:

The departure gate was filling up. It was a full flight, long haul. <u>His fellow pilgrims</u> included solo travelers taking a quick snooze or reading or making final changes on their laptops before boarding.

There is the ellipsis of the preposition phrase 'with his fellow pilgrims' in *The departure gate was filling up*, which can be presupposed with the reader reading forward. In this way, yet again, connections are established across the text.

Substitution

Sometimes, what is omitted (in the contexts of the noun phrase, verb phrase and clause) maybe be substituted by another form. These substituted forms vary depending on whether the substitution is in the context of the noun phrase (where for example, another shorter noun phrase may be used), verb phrase (where, for example, the verb *do* may be used) or the clause (where, for example, the adverbs *so* and *not* may be used). Halliday and Matthiessen (2004) suggest that ellipsis and substitution are 'variants of the same type of cohesive relation' (p. 563).

Let's look at the following section of the excerpt:

He scrolled through his history on his Facebook wall. It was <u>a time capsule that chronicled his thoughts, emotions, relationships, interests, life events, chats, pictures, wisecracks</u>. It was <u>a junkyard of his nonsense</u>, impulsively uploaded and conveniently timelined.

The noun phrase, *a junkyard of his nonsense*, substitutes for the much longer earlier noun phrase *a time capsule that chronicled his thoughts, emotions, relationships, interests, life events, chats, pictures, wisecracks*. The substitution here allows for conciseness as the much longer earlier noun phrase is condensed through the shorter and more impactful noun phrase *a junkyard of his nonsense*. To make sense of this shorter noun phrase, readers will need to look backwards to gather the relevant information, once again establishing cohesion.

Conjunction

Conjunction as a cohesive device includes the use of conjunctions (for example, coordinating conjunctions like *and*, *but* and *for*, and subordinating conjunctions like *when*, *because* and *although*) and conjunctive adverbs (like *however*, *nevertheless* and *then*) to create relationships and mark transitions within a text, establishing links and continuity within the text. Examples of relationships and transitions created through the use of conjunctions and conjunctive adverbs include cause and effect (signalled by, for example, *because*, *so*, *therefore* and *as a result*), condition (signalled by, for example, *if*, *unless* and *in that case*), concession (signalled by, for example, *although*, *while* and *nevertheless*), comparison and contrast (signalled by, for example, *but*, *however*, *in contrast* and *like*), and time (signalled by, for example, *since*, *when*, *during* and *meanwhile*).

There is rich use of conjunctions in the excerpt. Let's look at some instances of the coordinating conjunctions used in the excerpt:

> Many people dissed social media <u>but</u> to him this was life in 2D <u>and</u> his lifeline to the people who really meant something to him, no matter how tenuous those bonds were.

The use of the conjunction *but* serves to contrast the public view of social media and the protagonist's personal view of social media, and the use of the conjunction *and* serves to connect two aspects of social media that are important to him. In this way, the use of the coordinating conjunctions *but* and *and* creates logical flow.

The use of the subordinating conjunctions *as* is used in this sentence from the excerpt:

> He smiled <u>as</u> he came across a post or an Instagram of an event that he remembered fondly.

As mentioned in Chapter 5, the use of subordinating conjunctions creates subordinate clauses to main clauses. The use of the conjunction *as* creates the subordinate clause *as he came across a post or an Instagram of an event that he remembered fondly*, indicating and elaborating on the time (when) the main action of *He smiled* took place. As such, the use of the subordinating conjunction *as* creates a temporal relation between the main clause (main idea) and the subordinating clause (supporting idea), contributing to the smooth flow of ideas in the text, creating cohesion.

Repetition of Structures

When similar grammatical structures are repeated in a text, a rhythm or pattern is established within the text, unifying the text. In this way, cohesive ties are established within the text.

In the excerpt, repetition of structures (note: not repetition of words) are seen. There is the repetition of the structure *It was* in the following section of the excerpt:

> He scrolled through his history on his Facebook wall. <u>It was</u> a time capsule that chronicled his thoughts, emotions, relationships, interests, life events, chats, pictures, wisecracks. <u>It was</u> a junkyard of his nonsense, impulsively uploaded and conveniently timelined. <u>It was</u> his life in words and pictures shared with his 509 friends, 487 of whom would not even realise he was gone.

The cohesive devices of reference and repetition of structures are used concurrently here to establish a sense of continuity. The repeated structures, *It was*, start with the pronoun *It* which refers back to *his history on his Facebook wall*. While the repeated structures create a sense of rhythm and cohesion in the text, they also emphasise what is important to the protagonist – the documentation of his life.

Here is another instance of the repetition of structures in the excerpt:

> Past the metal detector and the X-ray checkpoints, he handed his documents to a lady in the signature sarong kebaya. Smile. <u>Boarding pass check</u>. <u>Name check</u>. <u>Passport check</u>. <u>Name check</u>. <u>Face check</u>. Welcome aboard. Smile. Next.

Not only is the verb *check* repeated, but the structure is also repeated – noun + verb (*check*). The subject is missing in these instances but we can infer that it is the airport staff mentioned earlier (*a lady in the signature sarong kebaya*) who is doing the checking. The repeated structures once again add rhythm and pattern to the text, creating cohesion. In addition, the repeated structures used in this way without explicit mention of the subject also conveys the impersonal, mechanical and business-like interaction between the protagonist and the airport staff, once again contributing to the airport setting of the narrative. In this way, there is continuity and cohesion established in the text.

Cohesion and Coherence

From the discussion above, you will note that cohesion is an **internal** property of the text. Cohesion refers to the explicit lexical and grammatical links established within a text. The use of both lexical and grammatical cohesive devices within a text creates a text that is smooth, connected and unified, aiding with the comprehension of the text.

Coherence, on the other hand, is an **external** property of a text. Coherence goes beyond the surface level lexical and grammatical links within a text. Coherence is about the overall logic and sense of a text, that is, whether the text makes sense in terms of the identification of the purpose, (target) audience, context and culture of the text.

How are cohesion and coherence related then? A text that is cohesive in nature will likely be more coherent than a text that is not cohesive. When a text is smooth, connected and unified in terms of ideas, topics and themes, it is easier for a reader to identify the purpose, (target) audience, context and culture of the text. For example, the narrative *Take-Off*, analysed for lexical and grammatical cohesive devices, is highly cohesive, and in turn, coherent, as readers can make sense of the text given that the ideas and themes in the text are connected and unified. Readers can identify the purpose, (target) audience, context and culture of the text. The purpose of the narrative may be to explore the thoughts, emotions and experiences of the protagonist leaving for his studies in the United States, focusing mainly on the themes of change and 'being apart'. The target audience could be young adults interested in leaving home to pursue further education, or readers interested in relevant themes like change. The context is set in Singapore, and more specifically, in the airport. The text is also rooted in Singaporean culture, signalled by clues like *National Service* (which Singaporean males will have to undergo) and *a lady in the signature sarong kebaya* (the uniform of cabin crew on Singapore's national carrier, Singapore Airlines).

Cohesion as Meaning Making in Texts

This excerpt is the concluding chapter of *Where's Grandma*.

EXCERPT 7.3

> *Grandma walked up to me tonight and as she opened her mouth to call me, she froze. Her right arm was slightly raised. She stood there for a long moment, her head tilted to one side as if she was trying to hear something. Her eyebrows were knitted on her wrinkled forehead.*
>
> *I knew she was trying to recall my name. 'What would you like Luke to do, Grandma?' I asked, breaking the spell.*
>
> *'Yes, Luke. Luke,' Grandma nodded. 'I wasn't to go back to my room.'*
>
> *She walked towards the kitchen hesitantly. I got up from the sofa and guided Grandma back to her room.*
>
> *Grandma squeezed my hand affectionately as we reached the doorway, just like she used to do every day when we came home from school.*
>
> *Over the past month, her condition has stabilised with the supplements and medication, but I know Alzheimer's disease is currently incurable. Grandma's memory will keep fading.*

> *Sometimes I ask myself: 'When Grandma's memory fades away, where will she be? Will she remember me?' I believe there is a part of her that will always remember me, just as Grandma will always have a place in my heart.*

This excerpt is highly cohesive with the use of several lexical and grammatical cohesive devices. Examples of the use of various cohesive devices are given below.

Repetition of Words and Phrases

The words *Grandma* and *Luke* are repeated to foreground the main characters in the narrative. The phrase *Grandma's memory* and the word *remember* are also repeated to emphasise the central aspects of the narrative, which are Grandma's memory loss and Luke's desire for his Grandma to remember him.

Synonyms

The verbs *recall* and *remember* are synonyms used in the excerpt. This use of synonyms across the text, ties the text together, once again emphasising the idea of remembering, which Grandma struggles with.

Meronymy

The body 'parts' of Grandma, as a whole, is emphasised in the first paragraph of this excerpt – *mouth*, *arm*, *head*, *eyebrows* and *forehead*. Not only does meronymy used in this way add to the unity of the text, the use of meronymy also helps readers visualise Grandma. There is another relationship of meronymy in the excerpt with parts like *room*, *kitchen* and *sofa* of the whole, which is the house. Readers are also able to then visualise the setting of this scene.

Lexical Set

There are a number of lexical sets that may be identified in this excerpt that are related to the core themes or aspects of the narrative. Here is a lexical set that relates to a core theme of the narrative, which is Alzheimer's disease as a disease that robs your memory – *Alzheimer's disease, recall, supplements, medication, incurable, memory, fading* and *remember*.

Structurally Related Words

In the excerpt, the words *fading* and *fades* are structurally related, with the root word being *fade*. The use of these structurally related words once again emphasises a critical aspect of this narrative, that is, Grandma's fading memory.

Reference

The use of reference as a cohesive device is strongly seen in the first paragraph of this excerpt.

> <u>Grandma</u> walked up to me tonight and as <u>she</u> opened <u>her</u> mouth to call me, <u>she</u> froze. <u>Her</u> right arm was slightly raised. <u>She</u> stood there for a long moment, <u>her</u> head tilted to one side as if <u>she</u> was trying to hear something. <u>Her</u> eyebrows were knitted on <u>her</u> wrinkled forehead.

A co-referential chain referring back to Grandma as the referent is set up with the use of the personal pronoun *she* and the possessive determiner *her*. Continuity and unity of reference to one of the main characters, Grandma, is established this way.

Ellipsis

There is an instance of ellipsis in the excerpt (marked by brackets) that prompts readers to look forward for the missing information:

> *Over the past month, her condition has stabilised with the supplements and medication (. . .), but I know Alzheimer's disease is currently incurable. Grandma's memory will keep fading.*

The missing information, the preposition phrase 'for Alzheimer's disease', may be retrieved by looking forward. In this way again, cohesion is established.

Conjunction

There is the use of coordinating and subordinating conjunctions in this excerpt to create relationships between clauses to connect ideas and create a flow in the text.

Let's talk about the use of coordinating conjunctions first, as used, for example, in the following excerpt:

> *I got up from the sofa <u>and</u> guided Grandma back to her room.*

The coordinating conjunction *and* not only adds another action but sequences the actions, that is, Luke first got up from the sofa and then guided Grandma to her room.

Let's take a look at another example:

> *Over the past month, her condition has stabilised with the supplements and medication <u>but</u> I know Alzheimer's disease is currently incurable.*

In this sentence, the coordinating conjunction *but* sets up contrasting ideas – although Grandma's condition has stabilised, Luke knows that the disease is incurable. The use of coordinating conjunctions helps to create different relationships between main clauses, that is, main ideas.

Next, let's look at an example of how a subordinating conjunction is used in the excerpt:

> *Grandma walked up to me tonight and <u>as</u> she opened her mouth to call me, she froze.*

The subordinating conjunction *as* is used to create a relationship of time between the main action in the main clause and the subordinate action in the subordinate clause. The main clause is *she froze* and the subordinate clause is *as she opened her mouth to call me* (note: there are two main clauses in this sentence – *Grandma walked up to me tonight* and *she froze*, linked by the coordinating conjunction *and*). The use of the subordinate clause with the subordinating conjunction *as* establishes when Grandma froze. In this way, ideas are connected in the text.

Repetition of Structures

There is an instance of the cohesive device of repetition of structures in the following:

> *I believe that there is a part of her that <u>will always remember me</u>, just as Grandma <u>will always have a place in my heart</u>.*

These repeated structures in the last line of the narrative not only provide a rhythm to the text, creating a flow within the text, they also emphasise the deep and lasting relationship that Grandma and Luke have.

This text is clearly highly cohesive, and in turn, coherent. A reader can make sense of this text and identify the purpose, target audience, context and culture of this text, aided by the use of cohesive devices that unify the text. The purpose seems to be to share Luke's experiences living with his Grandma who has Alzheimer's disease, focusing on the implications of this disease, primarily the loss of memory and perhaps relationships. The target audience seems to be young people with family members suffering from Alzheimer's disease or those who enjoy reading narratives on family relationships. The context is that of the home – clearly established though cohesive devices like meronymy. The text reflects a culture of family bonds, respect for elders and coping with an illness.

Exploring Cohesion with 15-Year-Olds

To help students better appreciate the importance of choice in language, I used an analogy of how grammatical cohesive devices are like brush strokes and lexical cohesive devices like the colourful paints that make up a painting. The more effectively these elements are combined, the better the painting/writing would be.

This excerpt from Tasha's reflection does effectively encapsulate the essence of cohesion in language. This analogy underscores the significance of understanding and using cohesive devices in writing. Just as a painter carefully selects brush strokes and paints to create a cohesive and coherent piece of artwork, writers must similarly employ grammatical and lexical cohesive devices to construct cohesive and meaningful written pieces. In this next section, we explore how Tasha and Norton, together with Masyita and Nathan, embarked on an ambitious eight-week journey to integrate the concept of cohesion (and adverbials) into reading and writing. This section of the unit on cohesion, which they also jointly constructed, was aimed at raising awareness of cohesive devices, recognising them in a text and applying them in writing through guided practice and planning.

In Chapter 6, we saw how the teachers incorporated an extract from *A True Good Thai* by Sunisa Manning as part of a larger unit of work to teach adverbials. To recapitulate, this story explores the journey of protagonist Det, together with his friends Lek and Chang, during Thailand's political upheaval from 1973 to 1976. The author weaves historical events and personal predicaments to shed light on the complexities of Thai identity and activism during this turbulent period in Thai history. The extract focuses on the moment when Det first meets Lek.

The choice of an Asian text as the model text to anchor this unit of work was deliberate as well. Tasha puts this very succinctly:

> It helps with the representation . . . for them [our students] to understand that Asians can use [the English] language well and can use the language in a sophisticated manner as well. Increasingly, people are recognising that Singaporeans are capable of using English in a far more sophisticated manner than previously. So I want the students also to be proud of the fact that as Asian, we are able to use English language for our own effective communication and with our own cultural, knowledge that's woven into our own expressions.
>
> (Tasha, interview)

Tasha and Norton explained that the aims for embarking on this unit of work was to address their students' struggles with cohesion and coherence in writing, ensuring paragraphs are free of irrelevant ideas and are logically linked. The teachers also wanted to work towards enhancing grammar instruction beyond language accuracy, utilising it as a tool for making meaning and content development to improve writing structure and flow. The following is the detailed plan which outlined the progression of activities over the course of four of the eight weeks set aside for this unit. These encompassed the following stages of thematic introduction, close reading, learning about cohesive devices, collaborative text construction and individualised planning for writing tasks.

1. **Introducing unit theme and writing task**
   - Students were introduced to the theme of the unit 'Describing people and places' and the descriptive writing task at the end of the unit.

2. **Close reading and annotating of text**
   - Students were guided through close reading and annotation of chunked sections of the model text, with teacher role-modelling to demonstrate how the writer described the characters.
   - Emphasis was placed on understanding the content and broader ideas regarding the writer's stylistic choices, highlighting how these choices contribute to cohesion and coherence.
   - Students were encouraged to visually demonstrate using an online interactive teaching and presentation tool to annotate details leading to their inferences about the text as they read together with their teachers.

3. **Learning about cohesive devices**
   - Students read and annotated the text again to learn about cohesive devices, focusing on lexical and grammatical cohesive devices such as repetition of words, meronymy, lexical set, reference, conjunctions and repetition of structures.
   - Prior to this, the teacher provided definitions of these devices, starting with lexical cohesive devices and then moving to grammatical cohesive devices.
   - Slides, including examples of repetition of words, meronymy and lexical set were used to aid understanding.

4. **Co-constructing of descriptive text**
   - Teachers worked with their classes to co-construct a descriptive text, demonstrating the application of concepts and skills taught through deconstruction of the model text.

5. **Planning descriptive text**
   - Students were given the opportunity to choose subjects they wanted to focus on and to plan how to use the cohesive devices taught to create their descriptive text in pairs. This task involved the description of characters.

As presented above, the teachers provided extensive resources for students, including activities such as close reading and annotating texts, learning about cohesive devices, co-constructing descriptive texts and planning writing. While

Cohesion and Coherence   141

the teachers spared no effort in creating these resources for their students, the section will highlight two of these:

Sample Activity 1

The following is the excerpt of *A True Good Thai* which the teachers used for closed reading and annotation of cohesive devices. Dividing this excerpt into several parts, the teachers asked questions to probe their students for understanding before embarking on the task to annotate cohesive devices.

EXCERPT 7.4

> *Just the head is a crowd of girls. One tall girl shrieks as she rolls a pealed longan in her outstretched hands. Thick strands of black hair cascade down her back and flow over her shoulders, reaching her ribcage. 'Don't make me eat it!' she cries.*
>
> *Look at her hands, slim and tapered. That upward turn at their tips, perfect for Thai dancing. Det watches the seniors push the 'eyeball' towards her. She chews it in front of her mouth, lips purse until she recognises the taste.*

Questions:

- How do you think the tall girl is feeling here? What details in the text tell you so?
- What activity do you think is the girl participating in? Why do you think is the girl in this situation?

EXCERPT 7.4 (CONTINUED)

> *Laughing, the seniors pulled a blindfold from over from her face. Det starts. She's Chinese. He can tell by the way they flock around her that they find her attractive too. She's brushing her hair out of her face, and turns her attention from person to person as she congratulates them on the trick. Their eyes meet; Det flicks his gaze up the beach.*

Questions:

- How do you think Det feels about the girl's identity? What details from the text suggest so?
- What could Det be feeling about the girl's physical appearance? What details from the text suggest so?

EXCERPT 7.4 (CONTINUED)

> *He climbs a low dune, brushes sand off a different log, straightens the crease of his pants. As he turns to sit, the girl appears. She presses her perfect hands*

together in a greeting and seats herself, tilting back with a sigh. The wind whips her hair into a small hurricane. She lets it fly, closing her eyes. Everything about her is long: long hair, long face that ends in a pointed chin, long limbs that seem to go on forever.

Question:

- In this paragraph, the writer provides more descriptions that paint the girl as someone whom Det finds to be attractive. Write down the relevant details from the paragraph that tell you so.

EXCERPT 7.4 (CONTINUED)

'What did they make you do?' she asks. Her eyes are deep black half-moons in a startlingly pale face. Though she speaks seriously, her cheeks create triangles that frame and lead his eyes to the peaked indent of her full top lip.

'I'm Lek,' she says, dipping her head. She speaks in flawless Thai with no twists of a Chinese accent. And she looks – she has a look of the lantom tree, the way it stands and the wind, sways and it's not broken. The arched branches; the oblong leaves, the spray of milky flowers with a deep gold drop.

'I'm Det.' He manages to sound unsure of his own name. He clears his throat, wondering if he should have snapped open his full name and title like an umbrella giving shade. Mom Laung Akarand, pleased to meet you, but call me Det.

Lek nods. 'Did you eat an eyeball too?'

'No,' he says. 'I'm sitting,' he adds, then winces.

Questions:

- 'What did they make you do?' she asks.
- What does the word 'they' refer to?
- What could the girl be trying to find out with her question?

This approach encouraged students to delve deeper into the text, analysing characters' emotions and motivations, which promoted deeper thinking and even empathy. The probing questions helped develop the students' ability to identify and interpret textual details, improving their comprehension and analytical skills. It fostered a deeper understanding of cultural and contextual nuances, enriching the literary experience. Additionally, the activity prepared the text for annotation, providing a structured way for students to engage with and reflect on specific elements, thereby enhancing their discussion and interpretation skills.

Sample Activity 2

In the explicit teaching of cohesive devices – in particular repetition of words, meronymy, lexical sets, reference and repetition of structures – the teachers were deliberate in explaining, demonstrating with examples (from the authentic text of choice) and then having the students apply these devices on their own. The following are samples from their teaching artefacts:

EXAMPLE A: ANAPHORIC AND CATAPHORIC REFERENCES

*Just ahead is a crowd of girls. **One tall girl** shrieks as <u>she</u> rolls a peeled longan in <u>her</u> outstretched hands. Thick strands of black hair cascade down <u>her</u> back and flow over <u>her</u> shoulders, reaching <u>her</u> rib cage. "Don't make me eat it!" <u>she</u> cries.*

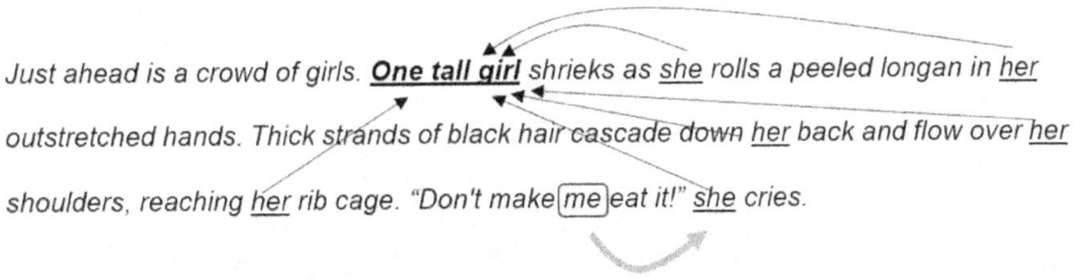

Figure 7.1 Anaphoric and cataphoric references in *A True Good Thai*.

Example A shows visually the concept of reference, that is, the act of referring to someone, an idea or a piece of information that has been mentioned before (anaphoric reference) or is about to be mentioned (cataphoric reference). In this sample, the instances of *she* and *her* refer back to *One tall girl* (anaphoric reference), while *me* refers forward to *she* (cataphoric reference), which in turn refers back to *One tall girl*. Such connections form a co-referential chain. This technique effectively illustrated for students how cohesive devices function in context, helping students understand their role in maintaining cohesion. By seeing these devices in action, students could better apply them to their writing, improving clarity and logical flow.

EXAMPLE B: REPETITION OF STRUCTURES

Look at the following uses of repetition of phrase and sentence structures in *A True Good Thai*. What structure is repeated in each case?

> Thick strands of black hair <u>cascade down her back</u> and <u>flow over her shoulders</u>, reaching her ribcage.

Answer:

- Verb + prepositional phrase
- Emphasising the movement of hair

> He <u>climbs a low dune</u>, <u>brushes sand</u> off a different log, <u>straightens the crease of his pants</u>.

Answer:

- Verb + noun phrase
- Providing details of Det's actions

To reiterate from the previous chapter, students had to work on the following writing task:

> **Topic: Describe a person whom you admire and the ways in which his/her appearance and actions show his/her personality.**
>
> You will be writing a descriptive essay of 350–500 words with a partner based on the above topic. Think of this task as creating linguistic snapshots/videos of a person whom you look up to.
>
> Consider the following questions:
>
> 1. Who is this person you will be describing? How is he/she related to you?
> 2. What do you admire about this person? Is it his/her personality, certain traits he/she possesses and/or his/her physical appearance?
> 3. What does this person look like?
> 4. What does this person sound like?
> 5. Where do you usually interact with him/her?
> 6. What is this person's body language and gait (how he/she walks, steps or runs) usually like?

The teachers identified and taught specific devices that they wanted their students to produce in their writing, that is, lexical cohesive devices, such as repetition of words, meronymy and lexical sets, along with grammatical cohesive devices like reference, conjunctions, and repetition of structures.

The collaborative efforts of Tasha, Norton, Masyita and Nathan in integrating the concept of cohesion into reading and writing have provided their students with a rich learning experience. Through an engaging exploration of cohesive devices, students were not only equipped with the tools to enhance cohesion and coherence in their writing but also gained a deeper understanding of the intricacies of grammar as a meaning-making resource. As Norton pointed out in his interview, cohesion is a vital aspect of writing often challenging for students, reflecting their struggles in linking and arranging ideas logically. This underscores the importance of teaching cohesive devices to help students express themselves effectively. In addition, Tasha's interview gave insights into the choice of using an Asian text like *A True Good Thai*, shedding light on the significance of diversifying classroom materials. By exposing students to different cultural contexts, the text not only sparked discussions on literary conventions but also encouraged exploration of a diverse range of customs and contemporary issues. This inclusive approach not only enhances students' cultural awareness but also fosters a deeper engagement with the text. In sum, the teachers' deliberate focus on cohesive devices has enabled their students to be more confident in using a variety of cohesive devices to improve on their written pieces.

Norton in his interview sums up their efforts very nicely:

> Our students often struggle with linking, arranging and presenting ideas in a logical and understandable, comprehensible manner. So by giving

them the tools in this particular unit to describe and to also put their ideas in a specific order, is definitely very important . . . it's definitely a very useful set of tools and strategies to get them to see this is how they can structure their thoughts and how these tools can help them to do that more effectively. So, to me, it doesn't just impact them positively on their writing, but also generally in the way they think.

(Norton, interview)

Extract Used in Chapter 7

The following is the extract from *Take-Off*, written by Dennis Yeo.

His mind was in a whirl. This next step was the culmination of his life up to this point. He could feel all his years converge and the planets line up. His was the typical Singapore success story, from the time he got into the Gifted Education Programme, to his clinching a coveted scholarship to study Computer Science in Stanford, in the heart of Silicon Valley. All the years of hot-housing in tuition enrichment centers had finally paid off. He could not even believe it himself when he tore open the envelope and read

> *APPLICATION FOR ADMISSION*
> *Congratulations! I am pleased to inform you that you have been selected for admission to the Degree (Computer Science) programme as a full-time student. Please confirm your acceptance of our offer of admission online. Requests for deferment will not be considered. Candidates who are unable to commence their studies will have to re-apply for admission as fresh applicants. We look forward to having you as part of the student community at Stanford University.*

The future was so sure and yet so uncertain. Things happened so quickly after that. Enrolling online, arranging accommodation, securing bank loans, shopping for winter clothes, having farewell dinner after farewell supper and stuffing every possession and memory one could carry into a suitcase that was now on a conveyor belt heading towards the cargo hold of the belly of an aircraft. Leaving home was both difficult and exciting. He felt like a ship that had cast off its moorings, sailing off towards a destination that lay beyond the horizon, knowing it was there but not actually seeing it.

He stopped at a huge globe that dominated the entrance of Planet Traveller. He would be further than he had ever been from home, almost a third of the circumference of the Earth. A couple kissing in a corner caught him stealing a glance in their direction. He liked how airports normalised all public displays of affection. Anyone watching would just assume that this would be the last time in a long time they would see each other so any physical contact was not just nudgingly accepted, but quietly envied. He thought of her. How would this affect them? He had heard how difficult it was to maintain a long-distance relationship. Three years apart, maybe four. Yes, he would return, but things would be different. They both knew that this would tear them apart, but none dared to say it to the other, preferring instead to say what the other wanted to hear. Sweet nothings of how they would whatsapp every day, how she would fly over and visit, how much they would miss each other, how what they felt would not change. Whoever said that absence made the heart grow fonder was a liar. Somehow, the physical body has to be present for someone to be fully and always remembered. She would meet some hunk at NUS and he would be there for her while he was 'virtually there'. Maybe he would meet someone too, a hot ang mo girl perhaps. The only constant, besides change, was that life would move on.

The one thing he knew he would certainly miss was the food. In Singapore, food was everything. It was why Singaporeans who complained ceaselessly about the country never packed their bags to migrate. It did not matter whether we ate to live or lived to eat but eat we did. Our 24/7 coffee shops boasted patrons at any time of the day. We greeted each other by asking if we had eaten regardless of what language we used or what ethnicity we came from. We described our culture as being 'rojak' because we really did not have any; we had many. What was the point of having a unifying culture if it meant waking up every day to green eggs and ham. Here in Singapore he was spoilt for choice. Singapore was a smorgasbord of international cuisine but what he would really crave for would be chye tow kuay, chwee kuay. roti prata telur bawang, teh tarik, mang jang kuay, Milo Dinosaur, Tiong Bahru porridge, mee siam, bak chor mee pok tah, chee cheong fun and a cup of Michael Jackson. I am sure the Americans would stare at him in disbelief. 'What? A cup of Michael Jackson?'. He laughed to himself, then frowned. He would not be able to eat any of these local delicacies once he was there – the authentic versions, at least.

What would his last meal be before facing an eternity of McDonald's breakfasts? He wanted noodles but he knew he would be hungry later. 'Airline food' was an oxymoron. Hainanese chicken rice it would be then – boneless 'white chicken', fragrant rice, chicken broth with a dash of minced garlic chilli sauce, pounded ginger and black soy sauce. Spicy, sour and sweet, just like life. As he ate, he looked back at what he would miss and looked forward to what he would experience. He knew friends who would not eat the skin of the chicken because it was unhealthy but what was the point of eating chicken if you were not going to eat the chicken skin, which was, to him, the best part of eating chicken in the first place. He relished the mingling of tastes in his mouth and bit into the succulent flesh of chicken and remembered something from his Literature class — 'to live deep and suck the marrow out of life'. That's what he would do. Seize each day. Make the most of every opportunity. Live with no regrets. Live to experience everything life had to throw at him. He cleaned his plate and with a lingering aftertaste of ginger, stood up and put on his earphones.

He still had time to kill.
 Another turning point, a fork stuck in the road

He zoned out.
 Time grabs you by the wrist, directs you where to go

He wandered around aimlessly for a while.
 So make the best of this test, and don't ask why

He checked his departure gate and double checked his boarding time.
 It's not a question, but a lesson learned in time

Yup his passport was still there.
 It's something unpredictable, but in the end is right

The shops were closing. Might as well head to the gate.
 I hope you had the time of your life

He went onto his wifi. What else did people do these days when they had nothing else better to do? Thank God for the Internet. If he had lived three decades earlier, communication by aerogramme would have taken two weeks. A trunk call just to hear a disembodied voice would have been ridiculously costly. Now with video calls and Facetime, you could see the person, hear the person, everything except touch the person. You were virtually there, except that you were not. You sometimes caught yourself touching the screen wanting to penetrate the distance and make contact. But it was not just the impenetrability of the screen. It was also the loss of that shared experience, the daily-ness of living, the separation that creeps in as people get used to not having you around. Your Skype calls become interruptions to their routine. There is nothing to say. Talk about the weather. Stay warm. Are you eating well? Sleeping well? Random people would walk past the screen say 'Hi!' then go back to whatever they were doing. Instead of feeling connected, you begin to feel more estranged. Humans always have a way of finding a way to do without someone.

He scrolled through his history on his Facebook wall. It was a time capsule that chronicled his thoughts, emotions, relationships, interests, life events, chats, pictures, wisecracks. It was a junkyard of his nonsense, impulsively uploaded and conveniently timelined. It was his life in words and pictures shared with his 509 friends, 487 of whom would not even realise he was gone. He wondered how things would be different between him and his friends. He smiled as he came across a post or an Instagram of an event that he remembered fondly. Many people dissed social media but to him this was life in 2D and his lifeline to the people who really meant something to him, no matter how tenuous those bonds were.

He typed 'I am outta here. See you on the other side.', hit the Enter button, logged out and joined the queue at the boarding gate. He was travelling light, just a haversack with his laptop in it, and a winter jacket, in case it was cold when he arrived. Past the metal detector and the X-ray checkpoints, he handed his documents to a lady in the signature sarong kebaya. Smile. Boarding pass check. Name check. Passport check. Name check. Face check. Welcome aboard. Smile. Next.

The departure gate was filling up. It was a full flight, long haul. His fellow pilgrims included solo travelers taking a quick snooze or reading or making final changes on their laptops before boarding. He remembered his first flight on his own without his family on a China Airlines flight bound for Taiwan for an in-camp training during his National Service. Around him were also couples inextricably entwined stealing pecks oblivious to anyone around them, and families with father and mother confirming if they had switched off the hall lights as their children looked out the glass at the humongous bird. He had to SMS his dad. His dad did not use a smartphone.

Hi Dad! Boarding soon.
Don't worry about me
ok? I will be fine. Send
Mum my love. I will
SMS you immediately
when I touch down.
Cheers!

Reference list

Halliday, M.A.K., & Hasan, R. (1995). *Cohesion in English* (14th impression). Longman.

Halliday, M.A.K. & Matthiessen, C.M.I.M. (2004). *An Introduction to Functional Grammar* (3rd ed.). Routledge. https://doi.org/10.4324/9780203783771

Yeo, D. (2019). *Take-Off*. Unpublished.

8 Conclusion

Introduction

As we draw this book to a close, we reflect on the core aim that has guided our journey all through these pages – demonstrating how grammar can be a powerful pedagogical tool for meaning making in the English language classroom. Throughout the chapters, we have endeavoured to make explicit the connections between grammar as a meaning-making resource and the development of literacy skills. A seminal study by Myhill and her team (2012, 2013) underscores the efficacy of contextualised grammar teaching, revealing the transformative potential of integrating grammar seamlessly into writing lessons. This empirical evidence highlights the pedagogical imperative of aligning grammar teaching with literacy demands reinforcing the intrinsic value of grammar as a dynamic meaning-making resource within diverse textual contexts.

We have emphasised how grammatical choices shape meaning, by embracing a 'descriptive' view of grammar. This is in contrast with the prescriptive approach that focuses solely on correctness. By adopting this descriptive stance, we encourage educators – teachers, teacher educators and pre-service teachers – to view grammar as a flexible tool for expression rather than a rigid set of rules. As Carter and McCarthy (2006) assert, this understanding of grammar as both structure and choice is essential for effective English language teaching. In presenting both grammar as structure and grammar as choice, we offer a comprehensive framework that bridges practical knowledge with practical application, always emphasising the critical links to literacy skills.

One of the key features of this book is the use of authentic Asian texts to illustrate how grammar and structure can be employed as grammar as choice in real-world writing. It is our hope that by incorporating familiar contexts, cultures and shared values, these texts can facilitate deeper understanding and connection for students as this cultural familiarity not only makes the learning process more engaging but also reinforces the relevance of grammar in their everyday lives.

The chapters in this book include a wealth of practical teaching ideas and materials. These resources, such as lesson outlines, activity ideas and teaching

DOI: 10.4324/9781003255963-8

strategies, have been contributed by teacher practitioners who have successfully integrated grammar as a meaning-making tool in their English language classrooms. These contributions, alongside their interviews and written reflections, offer valuable insights into the effectiveness of these approaches in real classroom settings. For all of these, we are truly grateful to the 10 teachers who have journeyed with us.

The remaining sections of this chapter will explore our proposed model of English language teaching and learning, examine the role of Asian texts and discuss the benefits and challenges of adopting this approach of grammar as a meaning-making resource for literacy development.

A Proposed Model of English Language Teaching and Learning

In designing this model of language teaching and learning (Figure 8.1), we drew inspiration from our work with our teacher-collaborators, synthesising the different ways in which they integrated grammar into their teaching practices. Within this framework, grammar assumes a pivotal role, transcending its traditional depiction as a mere set of rules. Instead, it emerges as a dynamic and impactful force, shaping both receptive and productive language skills. By recognising the capacity of grammar as a potent meaning-making resource, we underscore its significance in fostering effective literacy development within the language teaching and learning environment.

Throughout the instructional process, grammar emerges as a significant tool for both comprehension and expression. In the initial stages, when students engage with texts that require them to employ the receptive skills of listening, reading and/or viewing, grammar acts as a lens through which they decipher and interpret language. Teachers leverage grammatical structures within texts

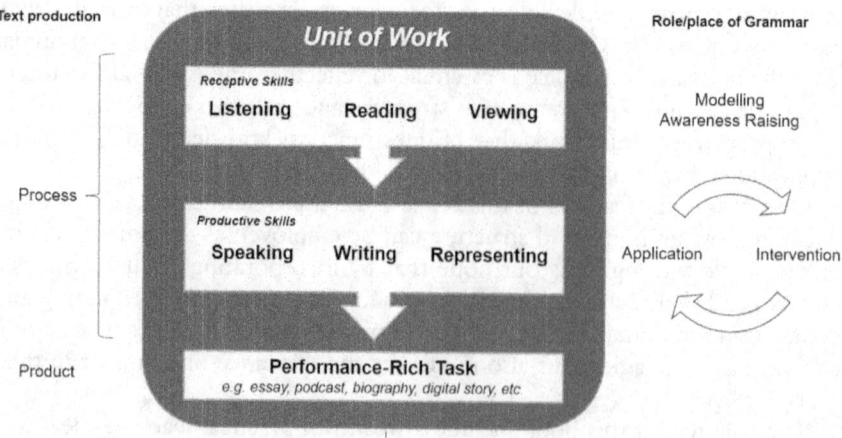

Figure 8.1 The role and place of grammar in teaching and learning.

to demonstrate how grammatical choices convey meaning, emphasising its role as a fundamental aspect of communication through texts.

In the latter stages of this model, emphasis is placed on the practical application of grammar during the production stage, which is crucial for students to grasp how grammar functions in authentic contexts. As students transition from receiving input to generating language output, they are encouraged to apply their understanding of grammar in authentic situations outlined by a teacher-designed performance-rich task. This could be an essay, podcast, digital story, video documentary and so forth. This application-oriented approach allows them to see first-hand how grammar influences their ability to effectively communicate ideas and concepts. Teachers design activities and tasks that require students to use grammatical structures in meaningful ways, fostering a deeper comprehension of how grammar operates in authentic language use.

However, recognising that some students may encounter challenges in applying grammar concepts independently, the model also incorporates intervention strategies during the production stage. If students struggle to effectively utilise grammar in their text production, targeted intervention lessons are provided to address specific areas of difficulty. These interventions serve to reinforce grammar concepts, clarify misconceptions and provide additional practice opportunities, ultimately supporting students in their journey towards linguistic proficiency.

By integrating application and intervention into the production stage of the model, students are afforded the opportunity to not only understand grammar theoretically but also to master its practical application in real-world communication scenarios. This approach not only enhances students' language skills but also equips them with the confidence and proficiency needed to navigate various linguistic contexts with ease. In essence, grammar goes beyond its traditional role as a set of linguistic conventions. Instead, it emerges as a vital tool for making meaning, deeply intertwined with every aspect of language learning and communication. By highlighting the intrinsic connection between grammar and meaning, this model underscores the transformative impact of grammar teaching on language proficiency and communicative competence.

Use of Asian Texts

In English language education, where grammar is fundamental to literacy development, integrating authentic texts has become prominent for fostering meaningful learning experiences. The incorporation of Asian texts into grammar teaching adds another dimension to English language teaching in Asian classrooms and emerges as a powerful strategy, imbuing lessons with cultural richness and relevance. By leveraging these culturally diverse texts, the teachers were able to enhance their students' understanding and appreciation of grammar while cultivating deeper engagement and linguistic proficiency within broader literacy development goals. This approach presents a compelling method for enhancing English language education, offering students a multifaceted learning experience that fosters cultural richness, deeper engagement with real-world language usage within diverse settings and increased exposure to linguistic variety.

HingMH's emphasis on the value of such texts underscores their ability to provide an immersive experience, bridging the gap between theoretical grammatical rules and practical application. By engaging with authentic Asian texts, her students were better able to gain a deeper understanding of grammar as a dynamic tool for communication, rooted in real-life situations and cultural nuances. Felice's observations further emphasise the importance of this connection, as students find familiarity and relevance in stories that reflect their own lived experiences.

Moreover, the integration of Asian texts not only enriches students' understanding of language but also nurtures cultural awareness and linguistic confidence. Tasha's remarks underscore the significance of representation, as Asian texts can showcase the diversity and sophistication of language use within the Asian context. By exploring texts that are contextualised in Asian culture, students can develop a deeper appreciation for the richness and complexity of their linguistic and shared cultural heritage. Gajen's perspective adds depth to this discussion, highlighting how Asian texts offer a unique lens through which students can explore their cultural identity and linguistic abilities.

Integrating Asian texts into grammar instruction provides a transformative educational experience, offering students a window into the multifaceted realm of language and culture. These texts serve as more than just teaching tools; they are conduits for exploration, discovery and empowerment. As educators embrace the richness of these Asian literature written in English, they can open doors to new possibilities for learning and growth. By weaving authentic Asian texts into grammar teaching and literacy tasks, educators equip students with the knowledge, skills and confidence to navigate the complexities of language in an increasingly interconnected world.

Benefits

Throughout our collaborative work with the 10 teacher-collaborators, we have gleaned insights from their interviews and written reflections, witnessing their remarkable journeys in the teaching and learning of grammar. In this section, we explore the impact of this paradigm shift on both teachers and students. By delving into the tangible benefits expressed by students and teachers alike, we hope to shed some light on the potential of integrating grammar as a meaning-making resource within the English language classroom.

Benefits to Learners

Teaching grammar as a meaning-making resource has impact on students' reading and writing development. By promoting awareness of the grammatical choices learners have and the varying impact of different choices, the students engaged in richer discussions about language use, rising above mere test performance. Moreover, scaffolded support in grammar teaching has made abstract concepts more tangible for many of the low readiness learners, fostering increased engagement and confidence with language use. The use of authentic Asian texts as models has exposed learners to more sophisticated language usage, enhancing their awareness of grammatical choices for impact.

The teachers also observed a significant shift in their students' engagement levels and understanding of grammar within this new framework. Departing from traditional approaches, the teachers embraced strategies that foster more meaningful and purposeful learning experiences. Many of their students developed a more holistic understanding of the role of grammar within reading and writing activities, empowering them to make better informed linguistic choices. This paradigm shift not only enhances language proficiency but also fosters a more enjoyable and meaningful learning journey for both teachers and students alike.

Benefits to Teachers

This innovative approach to grammar teaching has significantly enriched the teachers' professional development. Through targeted sessions, our teacher-collaborators have deepened their grammar content knowledge, empowering them to facilitate more effective literacy development. Furthermore, this pedagogical shift has enhanced their pedagogical content knowledge, providing a cohesive framework for integrating grammar into literacy contexts. By fostering reflection and reconsideration of teaching philosophies, this approach has prompted them to embrace a more contextualised approach to grammar teaching. The integration of grammar with other language skills has not only invigorated teaching practices but has also empowered the teachers to make informed pedagogical decisions, nurturing their students' literacy development more effectively.

Notable was the work done in the teaching of writing, where teachers recognised a need for a shift in the way writing was taught. This realisation led to a focused exploration of scaffolding techniques, including grammar intervention, aimed at supporting learners throughout their writing journey. By offering carefully crafted and structured assistance and facilitating collaborative drafting sessions, the teachers observed tangible improvements in their students' writing proficiency. The emphasis on scaffolded support was notably highlighted by teachers like Tasha, TAnne, Gajen and HingMH, who emphasised its crucial role in effectively nurturing their students' writing skills.

The integration of grammar as a meaning-making resource has, in a small way, impacted the 10 teachers working with us – in their views and collective stance towards the place of grammar in English language teaching and learning. From enriching their professional development to empowering their students' literacy development, this approach has effected a change in mindsets.

Norton so eloquently encapsulated the essence of what we were trying with the teachers on this journey:

> It's really a lot reflection, a lot of brainstorming and trying different strategies [to infuse grammar in the teaching of writing] . . . collaborating with the other teachers on how we can do this to make it more meaningful . . . To me, it's really a lot of self-improvement on my part as a teacher. And it really got me to reflect more on my teaching strategies and my philosophy in teaching certain aspects of language learning and teaching . . . It has also strengthened my understanding of the importance of grammar, not just about the nuts and bolts of language but also as a tool for meaning making because that is something that I didn't really think about, grammar as making meaning.
>
> (Norton, interview)

Challenges

Adopting grammar as a meaning-making resource in literacy classes marks a significant shift from traditional, isolated instruction to a more integrated and engaging approach. We have seen through the work of our teachers how effective this approach can be. However beneficial, this transition could present several challenges that educators must navigate to ensure effective implementation. The following sections describe five key challenges.

Professional Development Needs

Adopting a meaning-making approach to grammar teaching requires teachers to undergo significant professional development. This shift necessitates moving beyond traditional, rule-based methods to teaching grammar in context, emphasising how it contributes to overall communication and understanding. To facilitate this transition, continuous support from school leadership and policymakers is essential. Teachers need access to workshops and seminars. They will also require time set aside for collaborative planning sessions. Such professional development opportunities are crucial for equipping teachers with the skills and knowledge required to implement these innovative approaches effectively.

Curriculum Integration and Planning

Integrating grammar teaching within literacy activities involves meticulous planning and resource allocation. Teachers must design lessons that embed grammar seamlessly into broader literacy curriculum, treating it as a tool for enhancing understanding. This process demands appropriate resources, such as updated teaching materials that align with the new instructional methods. Schools may need to invest in new resources and digital tools to support this integration. Moreover, teachers must balance these innovative approaches with the need to meet established curriculum standards/learning outcomes and assessment requirements. This alignment is particularly challenging in jurisdictions with set curricula and prescribed textbooks, requiring careful planning to ensure new methods adhere to existing demands.

Resistance to Change

Some teachers may resist moving away from traditional grammar instruction methods. Overcoming ingrained pedagogical practices and facilitating mindset shifts require significant effort and time. Demonstrating the benefits of teaching grammar as a meaning-making resource can help in convincing reluctant teachers. It involves showcasing how this approach enhances student engagement, improves comprehension and results in more effective written pieces. Continuous support from school leadership is crucial in this regard. School leaders need to be convinced of the value of these innovative approaches and provide the necessary encouragement, resources and professional development opportunities to help teachers adapt to the new methods.

Diverse Learner Needs

Addressing the varying readiness levels and abilities of students presents a significant challenge. Implementing a one-size-fits-all approach to grammar teaching is ineffective given the diverse backgrounds and learning needs of students. Teachers must assess individual needs and tailor their instruction to ensure all students can engage with grammar meaningfully. Providing scaffolded support that caters to the varying abilities of learners requires thoughtful planning and differentiation. This involves creating lesson plans that offer the right level of challenge and support for each learner. Effective differentiation demands additional time and resources and teachers need ongoing support to access a variety of instructional materials to meet the diverse needs of their students.

Metalanguage Accessibility

Making grammatical metalanguage accessible to all learners, especially those with low readiness levels, involves simplifying complex terms without losing academic rigour. Teachers must find ways to explain technical concepts in relatable and understandable terms. This balance is crucial to maintaining the academic depth necessary for students to develop a more profound understanding of grammar. To achieve this, teachers need to employ creative strategies, such as using visuals, songs, hand signs and connections to students' prior knowledge. These strategies make metalanguage more comprehensible and palatable while aligning with the meaning-making approach. Thoughtful lesson design and innovative instructional techniques are essential to making grammatical concepts accessible to all learners.

Addressing all these challenges is vital for successfully integrating grammar as a meaning-making resource in a literacy curriculum. With the necessary support and careful strategic planning, educators can transform grammar teaching into a more dynamic and engaging component of language learning.

Concluding Words

As we conclude this book, we reflect on the transformative journey of reimagining grammar as a dynamic tool for meaning making in literacy development. Our exploration has demonstrated that grammar, when integrated contextually, transcends its traditional role and becomes vital for literacy development. Supported by empirical evidence and practical experiences, this shift emphasises grammar as a powerful means of expression and understanding rather than just a set of rigid rules.

We have shown how a descriptive approach to grammar – focusing on both structure and choice – can enhance language teaching and learning. Authentic texts, especially from Asian contexts, enrich the learning experience by making grammar teaching more contextual, engaging and relevant. This cultural connection, as we have seen, bridges theoretical concepts with real-world application, fostering a deeper appreciation of language.

Our work with teacher-collaborators has highlighted the significant benefits of this approach. Their students experienced enhanced engagement and comprehension, while the teachers found renewed purpose and professional growth. Despite challenges such as time constraints, the need for professional development and curriculum integration, the rewards to both teachers and their students have made this endeavour worthwhile.

As we move forward, we encourage you to embrace grammar as a dynamic resource for meaning making as our teachers have. By continuing to innovate, collaborate and reflect on our practices, we can make learning more meaningful for our learners. This book is a testament to the transformative power of grammar in English language teaching and learning, inspiring us to rethink and enrich our teaching methods. Together, we can create a more effective and inclusive language learning environment, fostering linguistic proficiency and deeper literacy skills in our learners.

References

Carter, R., & McCarthy, M. (2006). *Cambridge Grammar of English*. Cambridge University Press.

Myhill, D.A., Jones, S.M., Lines, H., & Watson, A. (2012). Re-thinking grammar: The impact of embedded grammar teaching on students' writing and students' metalinguistic understanding. *Research Papers in Education, 27*(2), 139–166.

Myhill, D.A., Jones, S.M., Watson, A., & Lines, H. (2013). Playful explicitness with grammar: a pedagogy for writing. *Literacy, 47*(2), 103–111.

Index

'A Weakness for Chocolate' (Wong) 46–47, 49–50, 68
ability 66
action research 5, 46
action verbs 51
active voice 71
adjective phrases 15, 16, 36
adjectives 27; form 14; function 14–15; meaning 14; as premodifiers 36–41, 43
Adrift: My Childhood in Colonial Singapore (Wong) 32–33
adverbials 107–118
adverbs 27; form 15; function 15–17; meaning 15
Alsagoff, L. 51
Amazing Komodo Dragon (Kurniawan) 52–53, 81
anaphoric reference 128, 143
antonyms 124
articles 18, 130
Asian texts 5–6, 74–75, 93–94, 149, 151–152, *see also individual texts*
aspect 59, 67–70, 78–81; past perfect 68; past progressive 69–70; present perfect 67–68; present progressive 69
'At the Peranakan Dining Table' (Lee) 118
attitudinal past tense 64
authentic texts 1, 4, 26, 112, 117, 151, 156, *see also individual texts*

bare infinitive 55
'Basang-Basa sa Ulan' 94–95
base form 30, 55, 58
benefits 152–154; to learners 152–153; to teachers 153–154

Carter, R. 1, 149
cataphoric reference 128, 143
challenges 154–156; curriculum integration and planning 154–155; diverse learner needs 155; metalanguage accessibility 155–156; professional development needs 154; resistance to change 155
clauses: clause patterns and transitivity 100–109; definition of 84–87; as meaning making in texts 90–93
coherence 134–135
cohesion: coherence and 134–135; definition of 121; exploring 138–145; grammatical cohesive devices 127–134; lexical cohesive devices 122–127; as meaning making in texts 135–138
common nouns 11
comparative reference 130–131
complement 103, 106–108
complex sentences 88–89
complex-transitive verbs 103, 107
compound sentences 88
compound-complex sentences 89–90
conjunctions 27, 133–134, 137–138; form 23; function 23–24; meaning 22–23
conjunctive adverbs 86–87
contextualised grammar teaching 1, 3, 5–6, 94, 149, 153
coordinating conjunctions 22–24, 86, 133
copula verbs 101–102
countable nouns 11
curriculum integration and planning 154–155

Index 159

demonstrative determiners 18
demonstrative pronouns 19
demonstrative reference 129–130
descriptive text construction 140, 144
descriptive view of grammar 2, 156
determiners 27; form 18; function 18–19; meaning 17–18; as premodifiers 36–41, 43
direct object 103, 105–106
ditransitive verbs 102
diverse learner needs 155
'The Duck Thief' (Chia) 112–113, 118–119
dynamic verbs 53–54

ellipsis 131–132, 137
Evergreen Tea House (Wong) 42–43, 48–49

factual present tense 63
finite clauses 100, 105, 106, 107
finite verbs 57–59
form 4, 10, 99, 105; adjectives 14; adverbs 15; conjunctions 23; determiners 18; nouns 12; prepositions 21; pronouns 19–20; verbs 13, 54–56
function 4, 10, 100; adjectives 14–5; adverbs 15–17; clause patterns and transitivity 100–109; conjunctions 23–24; determiners 18–19; as meaning making in texts 109–111; nouns 12–13; prepositions 21–22; pronouns 20; verbs 13, 56–57
future time 63–65

grammar: adjectives 14–15, 27, 36–41, 46; adverbs 15–17, 27; conjunctions 22–24, 27, 133–134, 137–138; descriptive 2, 156; determiners 17–19, 27, 36–41, 43; exploring 111–116; as meaning making in texts 109–111; nouns 10–13, 27, 34–50; prepositions 21–22, 27; prescriptive 2; pronouns 19–20, 27; verbs 13, 54–56
grammar as choice 1, 3–4, 6, 149
grammar as structure 1, 4, 6, 149
grammatical cohesive devices 127–134
grammar content knowledge 1, 5–6, 48, 153

habitual present tense 62
Halliday, M.A.K. 13, 121, 128, 132
Hasan, R. 121
high-readiness 26
historic present tense 64
hyponyms 124–125
hypothetical future 65

imperatives 55
indefinite pronouns 19
indirect object 105–106
instantaneous present tense 64
interrogative determiners 19
interrogative pronouns 19
intransitive verbs 101
'The Island' (Lee) 74–75

Jones, S. 2–3

Kebaya Tales (Lee) 81–82

lexical cohesive devices 122–127
lexical sets 126, 136
linking verbs 51
listening 95, 97, 113, 150
literacy development 1–2, 5–6, 94, 150–151, 153–154, 156
literacy skills 1–2, 44, 93–94, 150; listening 95, 97, 113, 150; reading 1–2, 30, 44, 74, 96, 140; speaking 69, 94; writing 1–3, 31–32, 44, 76–77, 94–96, 114–115, 140
low-readiness 93, 96, 111, 153, 155
'Lyca Gairanod: Thank you, Jesus' (Ballesteros) 94–99

main clauses 84
Malaysian Flavours (Lee) 110–111
Matthiessen, C.M.I.M. 121, 128, 130
McCarthy, M. 1, 149
meaning 10; adjectives 14; adverbs 15; conjunctions 22–23; determiners 17–18; nouns 10–12; prepositions 20–21; pronouns 19; verbs 13
meaning making 1–2, 4–6, 149–150, 152–156; clauses and sentences as 90–93; noun phrases as 39–43; verb phrases as 72–74; words and word classes as 24–26
mental verbs 52
meronyms 125–126, 136

metalanguage accessibility 155–156
middle-readiness learners 44, 74, 78, 93, 114
modal auxiliary 13, 56, 60–61, 65–67
modality 59, 65–67
Myhill, D.A. 3, 149

non-finite participle clause 105, 106
non-finite verbs 57–59
nonsense words 28–32
noun phrases 34–36, 104–106; exploring 44–50; as meaning making in texts 39–43; postmodifiers in 37–38, 43; premodifiers in 36–37, 39–41, 43; structure of 46
nouns 27; form 12; function 12–13; meaning 10–12; as premodifiers 36–41, 43; from words to phrases 34–35, *see also* noun phrases

object 105–108
object complement 106, 107–108
obligation 66

passive voice 71
past perfect 68
past progressive 69–70
past tense 55–56, 64–65; attitudinal past 64; hypothetical future 65; past event 64; politeness past 65
past time 64–65
pedagogical knowledge 5, 48, 153, 155
pedagogical tools 1, 149
permission 66
personal pronouns 19
personal reference 128–129
phrases 34–35; noun phrases 34–50; verb phrases 59–62, 72–81
planned future event 64
politeness past tense 65
possessive determiners 18
possessive pronouns 19
possibility 66
postmodifiers 37–38, 43
premodifiers 36–37, 39–41, 43
preposition phases 100, 107
prepositions 27; form 21; function 21–22; meaning 20–21
prescriptive view of grammar 2
present perfect 67–68
present progressive 69

present tense 55, 63–64; factual present 63; habitual present 63; historic present 64; instantaneous present 64; planned future event 64
present time 63–65
primary auxiliary 13, 56, 59–60, 62, 65
probability 66
professional development 5, 153–156
pronouns 27; form 19–20; function 20; meaning 19
proper nouns 11

quantifiers 19

reading 1–2, 30, 44, 74, 96, 140
reciprocal pronouns 19
'Red, Amber, Green' (Wong) 79–81, 83
reference 128–131, 137; comparative 130–131; demonstrative 129–130; personal 128–129
reflexive pronouns 19
relative pronouns 19
repetition: of structures 134, 138, 143; of words and phrases 121, 134
resistance to change 155

saying verbs 51
sensing verbs 51–52
sentences: definition of 87–90; exploring 93–98; as meaning making in texts 90–93
simple sentences 87–88
speaking 69, 94
stative verbs 53
structurally related words 126–127, 136
structures, repetition of 134, 138, 143
subject 104, 106
subject complement 100, 101–102, 106–107
subordinate clauses 85–86
subordinating conjunctions 22–23, 86, 133, 137–138
subordination 87
substitution 132–133
S+V+O structure 101, 103
synonyms 123–124, 136
Systemic Functional Linguistics 3–4

Take-Off (Yeo) 122–123, 127–135, 145–148

teaching: contextualised grammar 1, 3, 5–6, 94, 149, 153; culturally relevant 4; pedagogical knowledge 5, 48, 153, 155; pedagogical tools 1, 149
tenses and time 59, 63–65, 73–74
to infinitive 55
transitive verbs 101–102
transitivity 100–109
True Good Thai (Manning) 116–117, 119–120, 133–143

uncountable nouns 11–12

verb forms 54–56; base form 55; of copula *be* 55; ed/-en participle form 56; -ing participle form 56; of irregular verbs 54; past tense form 55–56; present tense form 55; of regular verbs 54
verb phrases 59–62; exploring 74–81; as meaning making in texts 72–74; structure of 60
verbs 27; dynamic 53–54; finite vs non-finite 57–59; form 13, 54–56; function 13, 56–57; meaning 13; stative 53; types of meanings 51–53
voice 59, 70–71

Where's Grandma? (Lim) 6–7, 39–42, 72–74, 90–93, 109–111, 135–138
words and word classes: definition of 9–24; exploring 26–32; as meaning making in texts 24–26
writing 1–3, 31–32, 44, 76–77, 94–96, 114–115, 140

For Product Safety Concerns and Information please contact our EU representative GPSR@taylorandfrancis.com
Taylor & Francis Verlag GmbH, Kaufingerstraße 24, 80331 München, Germany

www.ingramcontent.com/pod-product-compliance
Lightning Source LLC
Chambersburg PA
CBHW061716300426
44115CB00014B/2720